How to Make Money in High School and College

Best Money Making Methods as a Teen and Student, Building Your Own Apps, Selling E-books, and More Easy Side Job Ideas

Clement Harrison

Do **NOT** continue reading before you watch this video... or you will regret it!

Step-by-step video training to write your cv with no experience

After completing this training you'll be able to kickstart your career by:

- Discovering 7 key focus points you need to know about cv's to become relevant for the job you're applying for
- How to format and structure your CV to make it look professional and easy-to-read
- The #1 thing to put in your cv profile to attract attention
- How you can leverage your hobbies and interest to become much more interesting for Hiring Managers & Recruiters

Writing a CV when you have no work experience can be challenging, but with the right approach, anybody can write a CV that will get them noticed by employers and land job interviews.

SCAN the QR-Code to access this must-watch video and set yourself up for the jobs you want

from various sources. Please consult a licensed professional before attempting any techniques outlined in this book.

By reading this document, the reader agrees that under no circumstances is the author responsible for any losses, direct or indirect, that are incurred as a result of the use of the information contained within this document, including, but not limited to, errors, omissions, or inaccuracies.

Table of Contents

Introduction

"I'm a great believer in luck, and I find the harder I work the more I have of it."

-Thomas Jefferson

This was a quote from one of the founding fathers of the United States, and I would say he was a pretty smart man. This quote is still relatable today and will certainly relate to what we will discuss in this book. The harder you are willing to work, the more opportunities will come your way. The more opportunities that come your way, the greater chance you have for positive results.

This book is written for high school and college students. While reading, you'll discover several ways to earn money on the side that will accommodate your schedule and allow you to use your skills. The market is actually saturated with side jobs, or side hustles, available for just about anybody, even if you have no particular skill set or work experience yet. One of the main reasons students have had difficulty maintaining work while going to school is they could not find employers who could work with their schedule. Those who did not have the benefit of getting help from family members often had to choose between work or school.

There is a better way. Imagine having numerous side hustles right at your fingertips that you can pick up and start doing today. If you have a free evening, work a few extra hours. If mornings are better for you, then that's also an option. If you have a few hours in between classes, then guess what? You can earn a few extra bucks. Does this sound too good to be true? Well, it's not. These opportunities do exist; people just are not aware of them.

This book Exposes these opportunities right here and now. In addition to the schedule convenience, there are a diverse number of jobs available, from online business to manual labor. Whatever may be your forte, there will be a side hustle available to you. There is a plethora of work available out there, and there are only two prerequisites: Have the ability to be flexible and possess a strong work ethic. One thing I am not promoting here is a get-rich-quick scheme. This is anything but that. You will definitely have to put your hours in.

Some Cold, Hard Facts

Being a student is not easy. On top of worrying about your studies, you have to contend with what you will do to pay off your loans after college. This becomes a financial burden for many adults as they spend the rest of their lives paying for their education. Short of getting their loans forgiven somehow, they will have to work them off. This is not easy to do, as the many numbers we go over will show you.

The statistics showing the student loan debt as of 2020 are astronomical. Around 45 million students are borrowing money to go to school. Their combined loan numbers equal around 1.6 trillion dollars (1.56 to be exact). This makes student loans the second-highest consumer debt category behind mortgage debt. As recently as 2018, the student loan debt for the average person was $29,200, which was a two percent increase from the prior year. This does not count the money to be paid in interest. (Friedman, 2020)

Having to pay these loans back is not the only issue. Student loans can affect your ability to buy a house or car, save for retirement, or pay for other emergencies. Many students either can't leave home at any point or have to move back with their parents, since they can't afford the student loans and rent at the same time. Since college students are just entering adulthood, many do not possess acute financial skills to keep their money matters straight. Depending on the type of career you go into, you could be paying off student loans for the vast majority of your life. Having this debt hovering over you is, at the very least, a nuisance.

This is a serious financial crisis, and until we figure out how to get rid of loans or reduce the cost of education, I don't see this issue resolving itself soon. This is not what we are here to discuss today. I want to help you from falling into the debt trap by being able to make some decent side income. Whether you want to be rich or not is beyond the point. If you don't, that is okay. I am simply here to show you how to be financially independent so you don't have to rely on anyone, whether it is your parents, siblings, friends, cousins, partner, etc.

Whether you care about making money or not, you will need to have it. On top of your student loans, you will have to worry about lodging, utilities, health insurance, food, gas, emergency funds, and many other financial obligations life will throw at you. It's nice to be able to handle all of these independently without seeking out help from others.

I personally experienced major financial matters thrown at me while I was a student. However, I was able to pay rent for an apartment near my work, buy temporary health insurance until my work's insurance kicked in, and get caught up on monthly bills before I even started my job. This is because I already had enough money saved up. It gave me a gigantic head start upon entering the real world.

Beyond reducing your debt, having a side gig or hustle will have a tremendous amount of benefits. It is truly a hidden treasure in the workforce. They will give you a major leg up during life in general. Here are some additional reasons to consider adding some side hustles into your life.

- It is empowering to have multiple sources of income. The traditional route in the past was to rely on one company to provide a living for you. Due to many changes in the economy, and the uncertainty that comes with relying on one paycheck, a person feels like they are in much more control when they have multiple sources of income. Imagine a scenario where you have five sources of income, whatever they may be. Now imagine losing one. You still have four others you can rely on and maybe even give more focus to. You will be able to focus more on the four remaining sources, and, since you are already in the side hustle mindset, you may be able to find another one easily.

- You can learn a new skill or several, and you may even be able to find a whole new career from it. Side hustles allow you to learn something without having to put all of your eggs into one basket. Imagine how many new things you can learn in this manner. This will become much more apparent as we begin discussing specific gigs.

- I have mentioned this already and will continue to point it out throughout the book, but saving money and gaining wealth is a major benefit here. You will learn the value of money and gain some amazing money management skills.

- Having side hustles to grow your finances will improve your stability. This will have a major positive impact on your mental health. Money, or a lack of it, leads to feelings of insecurity. When we have more money available to us, we are in a much better state mentally because we will have less fear and worry. I am not saying that money will cure mental health; numerous factors contribute to it. I am just suggesting it can ease the volatility of our minds.

Side hustles started off as small ways to make extra money. These gigs often lasted a short while until people could get back on their feet. Also, there was a very limited amount of side gigs available. With the explosion of freelance, independent contractors, and temporary work, these opportunities have grown immensely. Many individuals create full-time work and income from side hustles and never have to work a job with a regular schedule again.

How This Book Will Help You

Now that we have discussed the value of side hustles, how can this book help you? First and foremost, I will provide dozens of money-making ideas that will vary in skill level, experience, interest, time commitment, and of course, pay rates. This book will cover a wide diversity of gigs that you can start doing as soon as possible. If one idea does not work for you, there will be several others to choose from.

Not only will you discover numerous side hustles, you'll also learn how to get started and even the steps needed to find customers. I will help you stand out and entice the best clients for your work. At the end of this book, you will know how much you can charge for various jobs or projects so you can always earn what your skills are worth. I don't want you to feel shortchanged, nor do I want your clients to feel ripped off.

This book will not just contain a lot of theory. It also contains real-life stories from other people who have become successful side-hustlers. You will truly get to learn from experience. Finally, once you make that extra money, you will need to know what to do with it. There is no sense in making extra money if you are just going to spend it irresponsibly. Make that dough and use it to build a better and more stable life.

While I cannot prepare you for every single issue that may arise, after reading this book, you will be prepared to take on a new world. You will begin looking at money and work in a different manner. You will become the ultimate side-hustler and be prepared to diversify your work portfolio.

Who Am I?

I have been talking to you about my ideas, but I have yet to properly introduce myself. My name is Clement Harrison and over the years as a bestselling author and business owner of Muze Consulting, more than 200,000 people read my material to discover how to use psychology and systematic methods to unlock the door to business and personal success. That could mean finding a job you love, earning more money, starting your business or mastering the intricacies of your mind.

I started my business while I was studying Neuroeconomics at Princeton. Since I came from a family that did not have much money to spare, I could only afford college by paying it for myself. That's when I decided to discover how money makes the world go round.

While I was at college, I kept hearing all these "advices" from specialists in the field of finance and I found out that experts often tell you how to do something but *they never really follow their own advice.*

I was certain that there were better options to live a more rewarding life if we could use the way our mind works to concentrate on what is actually effective. Not just in business but also on a personal level: in health, social relationships, work, money management and more.

Since then, I've been testing and sharing my findings with the world via my business and books. I love what I do because I've made my living by helping people from all walks of life to become successful and thrive in today's world.

Chapter 1:

Neighborhood Jobs

A neighborhood is a community of people, homes, and businesses that make up a small living space within a region. As you walk around your own neighborhood, you will see children playing, people mowing their lawns, going out for walks, mingling with one another, and even doing community events together. A neighborhood is a place where you live within a certain set of rules, both morally and legally. There is a lot that you can see as you walk around your local community. However, there is something else I will bring to your attention, and that's opportunity.

That's right, opportunity. Your local neighborhood is filled with jobs and projects that need to be completed, and people are aching to have someone fulfill those needs. The variety of these jobs is endless. You may not know about them because you did not know where or how to look for them, but they really are everywhere. You probably have seen many people in your surroundings performing them already. The guy next door offering to shovel peoples' driveways for a small fee is performing a side hustle. The guy who lives in a big city block who moves peoples' cars for them is performing a side hustle. Many of your neighbors are taking advantage of the side hustle phenomenon, and I will showcase how you can too.

The great thing about neighborhood jobs is that you already know a lot of your potential clients. You may be friends with them, see them out and about, waved at them, or at least heard of them. You will not have to travel far to find decent work. One thing to consider is avoiding stepping on peoples' toes. Don't start stealing customers away from other people in your neighborhood. For example, if there is already someone doing landscape work for a particular house, find a different house to go to. Respect an individual's space. The last thing I want is for you to get into a neighborhood conflict.

Neighborhood Jobs

The book is geared mainly towards high school students, so I will be focused on jobs that are suitable for teens. Obviously, certain jobs and projects have age restrictions on them. As I break down individual jobs, I will provide as many details as possible so you can be informed. This section will break down the experience level and skills needed, working conditions, pros and cons, the average pay rate, etc. Once you learn of the many opportunities there are just on your own block, you will be thrilled to get out there and make some extra cash. Again, the most important requirement for any of these is that you are willing to go out there and do the work.

Dog Walker

Have you seen these kids walking around the neighborhood with about five dogs on a leash? If you are an animal lover, you probably think about how lucky they are. The truth is, those probably are not all their dogs. These people are actually working and making an income. Dog walking jobs are a thing, and people can make great money doing them while providing a wonderful service for the owners and the dogs. Dogs need exercise and fresh air, and owners often don't have the time to do it for them—at least, not as much as they would like.

If you are not an animal lover, this may become quite challenging. Enjoying the company of animals is certainly a large criterion that needs to be met if you choose this path. You will literally be surrounded by animals and the more money you want to make, the more exposure you will need. If you are an animal lover, then this side hustle may be right up your alley. Of course, this is not the only qualifying criteria. Not all people who love children should teach elementary school, and not all people who love dogs should be dog walkers. While no previous experience is needed to become a dog walker, there are many things you should take into account.

Before you jump into dog walking as a career, consider some of the pros and cons. Weigh all of these against each other and determine if the pros outweigh the cons. From here, you can decide to proceed forward or not. We will start by discussing the cons.

- First of all, you have to find clients. This is true of many side hustles, so you may not want to weigh this too heavily. However, people have strong relationships with their animals, which will make the process of finding clients who trust you quite difficult. Marketing yourself can become a full-time job on its own. Your best bet may be to start with people who know you well, and then they can let people know about you through word of mouth. Once people realize how good you are, many will seek you out on their own. I would also advise creating a website or at least going through various online platforms like social media to get the word out. Old-school methods like using flyers, emailing directly, or cold calls can also be beneficial. Whatever you decide to do, be proactive with your marketing. It does not matter how great of a job you do if no one knows about you.
- Your income will be variable and unpredictable. Unlike a regular job, where you receive a paycheck every pay period, dog walking income is not set nor guaranteed. Even if you build up a

steady number of clients, there is always the possibility of cancellations for whatever reason. Clients may move or decide they do not want your services anymore. There may be a reason why you can't personally perform the duties for a while. For example, you may get an injury. The bottom line is your income is never fully guaranteed, so take this into account. No matter how many clients you adopt, never ditch your marketing efforts, because you never know when you may need them.

- You may have to adopt the "rain, sleet, and snow" motto of the post office here. This means that inclement weather cannot always keep you from your duties. I am certainly not saying to go out when it is severely dangerous to do so. However, realize that the sun won't always shine brightly on your walks. To keep a steady income and maintain the trust of your clients, you must be consistent and not allow the weather to dictate your business. Buy some good snow shows, a warm coat, some gloves, and a hat, and keep on doing the side hustle. Here is something to consider: When the weather is bad, many people will refuse to go out. You may actually gain more clients because of your work ethic.

- Cleaning up messes can get, well, messy. If you have ever taken a dog on a walk, then you know how many messes you have to clean up. That is just one dog. Imagine having to do it for multiple dogs. It is certainly something you will get used to, but it can be off-putting at the beginning. If you have a weak stomach, proceed with caution.

- Dogs do not last forever. This can be a hard fact to take for those of us who adore animals. Over time, you will build a strong bond with a dog. At some point, the owners may move away, or the dog will inevitably pass. When this happens, it can be difficult to take. The pain will be major, but will eventually subside. Other great dogs will be in your life too.

- Animals can get quite wild. Even if a dog is well trained, they are still dogs and can lose control at any point. It is hard to tell how a dog will react to certain things, like other animals, noises, new sights, or people. It is essential always to be alert, no matter how familiar you are with a dog.

If you choose this as a side hustle, also consider becoming a pet sitter. You will have many more opportunities for work, and, with the skills you already possess as a dog walker, it will be a smooth transition for the most part. I hope I have not scared you away with the cons. There are numerous benefits that come with being a dog walker too. We will now go over some of the pros.

- I already mentioned the obvious one, and that is the fact that you will be around dogs all of the time. If you are a dog lover, you will be in heaven with all of your furry friends.
- You will meet many friendly people too. Inevitably, you will develop a relationship with the dog owners. As you get to know them, you will develop a bond over your love of animals. They will promote your business better than anybody if you do a good job.
- You will get plenty of exercise. In addition to walking, handing the tags will create a workout on its own.
- You will get plenty of fresh air and discover new parts of your city.
- Dogs love you unconditionally, and, when they are happy, it is almost impossible not to be happy yourself.
- Instead of dealing with office politics, drama, and complaining, you will be dealing with dogs licking your face. I know which one I would rather have.
- The schedule will be flexible. If you have more time early in the morning, then walk the dogs early in the morning. If you have more time in

the afternoon, do it then. Workout the best schedule between you and the clients and get going.

- Once you build up your business, you can make pretty good money and even more than what you would make working full time.

Before you attempt walking multiple dogs at a time, start with just one and move up from there. This is a great side hustle to get into and if it sounds like something you would like to get into, then let's get started finding some clients.

We mentioned before the power of word-of-mouth. This may be the most effective sales technique out there, and it's essentially free. People will just have to like you enough to be willing to talk about you. Other effective methods include community bulletin boards, social media pages, freelance websites like Thumbtack or Fiverr, dog-walking apps, and networking with other dog walkers. If your local community has a newsletter, definitely utilize it if you can. There are plenty of free and low-cost methods to advertise your services. Take advantage of all of them. If you already have a strong presence in your community, this will be a big advantage.

Timing can also be important. For example, people may be looking for dog sitters during major holidays or travel seasons. Use this time to find clients you can build a relationship with. If they are impressed by you, they will come back for your services.

Besides some advertising expenses, there are a few other expenses to take into account. You will definitely need some comfortable shoes and clothes for any type of weather. Consider the terrain that is near you. If you live near a lot of hiking trails and mountains, you should definitely have the shoes that will allow you to go on them. Of course, you will need some good leashes. You don't want to take a chance with a cheap leash, because it can easily break on you. This will create a whole other set of problems, including safety issues for you, the dogs, and the general public. You will also need bags to pick up dog poop. Finally, have a few dog-healthy treats on hand, just in case.

Once you start getting clients, remember that you are representing yourself and your new-found business. Make sure you are reliable, friendly, and hardworking. Be ready to answer questions and be somewhat flexible with clients' requests. You must be trustworthy, because people will be leaving their pets in your hands. This is a big responsibility that you must take seriously. Show up on time and do not cancel unless you absolutely have to. If you must cancel, give as much advance notice as possible. When you offer to walk a neighbor's dog, they depend on you so they can get other things done. Do not let them down.

The final thing we will discuss is payment. Dog walking is hard work and you certainly want to get paid for it. If there are other dog walkers in your area, try to find out what they are charging and stay competitive with your rates. The hourly rate will vary depending on the state and also the economic status of the community you are in. Of course, the last thing you want to do is price gouge people. The goal is to make money without taking advantage of people. According to care.com, the average hourly rate is around 16-18 dollars per hour. One benefit you can give to your clients, which will also be a great advertising technique, is to offer referral bonuses. This means you will save your clients money in some way if they bring you additional customers.

Dog walking is an exceptional side hustle and also very rewarding. If you love dogs and feel a special kinship with them, this gig may be right up your alley. If it's not, don't worry. There are several more opportunities we will go over.

Rating's System Summary:

Experience level: Zero to very low

Time commitment: Medium

Pay rate: $$$. You will earn a decent living if you are willing to put in the hours.

Car Washer

Car washing is a great side hustle, especially in the summer when the sun is out. Anyone in high school or college could have fun doing this job and would do well at it if they are motivated. What is one of the most common things you see when high school kids are trying to raise money for something? In many cases, it is a car wash. It seems like a natural transition for many to make this a summer job. The main qualifying criteria is that you pay attention to detail, you enjoy working with your hands, and you have a strong work ethic.

Washing cars is not an easy gig, especially when you start getting into detailing, waxing, and cleaning the interiors. One car can take several hours when you first get started. Don't worry, because you will get faster and more efficient with time. However, do consider the time commitment it will take when you start this side hustle. It will take a lot out of you, but being in that hot sun with water flowing all over you can be quite refreshing. If you love cars and are meticulous about keeping them clean, consider becoming a car washer.

Just like anything else, consider some of the pros and cons and weigh them against each other. If you are willing to put up with the negatives to bask in the positives, then it is time to get started. The following are some of the cons of starting a car washing business.

- It will be a seasonal business. At the very least, you will make the most amount of money during the warmer seasons and take major pay cuts during the colder seasons. Inclement weather will put a stop to your car washing on any particular day. People will not pay for car washes just so the rain, sleet, and snow can dirty them up again. Consider where you live and determine how profitable of a business car washing will be year-round.

If you live in San Diego, Phoenix, or Orlando, then chances are you will be able to make great money throughout the year. If you live in a place where poor weather dominates for several months, consider how much profit you will lose during these times. One way to offset this can be to work as much as you can during warm weather so you can afford to take days off during the cold.

While you certainly don't control the weather, clients will be upset if they constantly get their car washed, only to have it rain or snow later. Even though the weather is unpredictable, do your best to assess what it will be like for a couple of days and determine if washing a car is appropriate.

- There can be a lot of equipment involved if you are doing more than cleaning the exterior. This equipment can get expensive to repair or replace when it breaks.

- Finding clients can be difficult. There are many car washing and detailing shops around every corner. It is often easy to drive-thru quickly and get what is needed. You need to offer clients a reason to hire you. Providing service at their home is a good incentive.

- Damage to the car that occurs while you are cleaning it will become your responsibility. Even the smallest scratches and dents can hit your pocketbook in a strong way. Great care must be taken throughout the whole process to prevent damage from happening.

Consider these cons of starting a car washing business. We will now discuss the pros.

- It will be a great exercise. Anyone who has ever washed a car thoroughly knows how much manual labor is involved.
- With the various movements used for cleaning, detailing, and vacuuming, you will eventually work out your whole body.
- This will be a great cash business. As you increase your clientele, you will bring in a lot of income. You could potentially make hundreds of dollars a day. Take advantage of this when the weather is good.
- There is a lot of flexibility involved. If you have a regular job or go to school, you can take advantage of your days off by washing some cars. You can even do it in the morning, evening, or after work or school.

- Fresh air and sun are good for you, mentally and physically. You will get plenty of it as a professional car washer.
- You will get to meet some great people who will become your clients, and you will also get to see some great looking cars.

Assess these pros and cons and determine if you are choosing the right path for yourself. This is a great side hustle once you get started. Before you get your first client and even before you start advertising, there will be a few things you will need. While there won't be any overhead costs if you will be using either your clients' or your personal driveway, there are a few items you need to have.

First of all, you'll need a good hose that will stretch a long distance. You may be able to borrow one from the client, but there is no sense in inconveniencing them in this manner. It is better to just get your own. In addition, you need all of the supplies for cleaning and washing the exterior and interior. This includes something that is safe to use on the body of the car, plus something to clean the tires and wheels. You will also need a good window cleaner and something to take off the bug stains. Those can be pesky and difficult to remove. In addition, many products are needed to clean the interiors like the dashboard and placemats, as well as a good upholstery and leather cleaner. Finally, a solid vacuum that will also help you get into the hard-to-reach places in the car is essential.

Your initial investment may cost you a few hundred dollars, but you can make that up in a couple of days if you are busy enough. These supplies are needed so do not try to skip out on them. If you initially plan to clean the exterior only, then you don't need to buy all of the cleaners for the interior. If you want to increase your business and income potential, then cleaning the interiors is something you should eventually consider. However, starting with just the outside of the car is an excellent way to get your feet wet, both literally and figuratively.

Once you have the supplies you need, then it is time to market yourself. Be very clear about what services you provide. If you don't plan on doing interior cleaning yet, then don't advertise it. Use Facebook and other social media outlets to get the word out. Using Instagram to post pictures of clean cars is a good option too. If your community has a newsletter or bulletin board, then utilize those as well. Word of mouth will go a long way. If people are happy with your work, they will let other people know about you. So, do good work. Finally, keep your own car clean. If you are seeking out clients to clean their car while your own car is a mess, then your offer may not look so good on the surface. Always be professional, friendly, and fair when dealing with clients or potential clients.

Two or three cars in a single day is a good starting point. It is not simply rinsing the car off with a hose. You really have to get in there with a good rag or sponge and get into all of the crevices. The car must be shiny all around for the clients to be truly impressed.

Once you get quicker and more efficient, you can increase the number up to four or five and beyond in a single day. Determine how many cars you can clean in a single day while still doing a good job. Eventually, time factor will not be as important as the quality of your work.

A car washing side hustle can bring you in quite an income. You can either charge by the hour or the car. If you are only cleaning the exterior, then 10-15 dollars per car is a fair price. If you will also clean the interior, then 50-60 dollars per car is fair. If you plan on charging hourly, then anywhere between 20-25 dollars per hour is acceptable.

I failed to mention earlier one of the greatest things about doing a car wash side hustle, and that is the fact that you can wear your bathing suit while doing so. Ditch that work uniform for some swim trunks and flip flops. I would tell you to roll up your sleeve, but you won't have them if you're wearing a tank top or t-shirt. Whatever the case, get ready to make some money.

Rating's System Summary:

Experience level: Low. Basic knowledge of how different cleaners work is needed.

Time commitment: Medium. You will need to put in a decent number of hours to make a good extra income. If you can commit 10-15 hours in a week, then you can receive a part-time income.

Pay rate: $$$. Once you get a lot of business, you will be bringing in some good money.

Lawn Maintenance

A good way to make some extra income is by doing some old-fashioned yard work. Children figure this out pretty early as they are out there at a young age mowing their own lawns. Lawn care and maintenance are a great way to make some extra income, especially if you are willing to diversify what you will do. For example, you can mow lawns during the summer, rake leaves during the fall, do general clean up during the winter, and prune trees and bushes during the spring. While lawn care is seasonal to a degree, being willing to perform several different tasks will be a big plus for you.

This kind of work is a fit for any able-bodied teenager in high school and college. You can easily work on a few lawns over the weekend, or whatever your days off would be. If you enjoy manual labor and don't mind getting your hands dirty, then consider lawn care as a side hustle. When doing lawn care, one thing you need to be mindful of is going into someone else's territory. There are plenty of people who do lawn care and maintenance as a full-time career, so the last thing you want to do is take away their business. Focus on people who still need help and also stick to what you can do.

There are certain lawn maintenance and landscaping jobs that don't require a high level of skill, but there are others that do and may even require training and certification. For example, any type of plumbing or electrical work should be avoided if you do not have the experience to handle it. Also, building things like decks and fountains should only be done by professionals. Even work like pouring fertilizer or certain chemicals requires knowledge based on what is healthy for particular lawns and plants. Stick to work that involves manual labor like raking leaves, mowing the lawn, picking up debris, or cutting edges until you become more experienced with the science behind lawn care. There is a reason certain people's grass looks greener. It is not just the time they put in but the techniques they use too.

There are many pros and cons to starting a lawn care side hustle. As we go over these, determine if it's something you are willing to get into. We will start with the cons first.

- Major injuries are a possibility. I am not just talking about cuts, blisters, and bruises here. You could also injure your back, a limb, or any other vital part of your body. You will be handling some equipment that is dangerous too. Be well-prepared and do your research before you use any type of machinery.
- You may have to work with many different chemicals. Be careful about over-exposure and avoid staying in restricted spaces while using them. Also, take great caution to prevent getting these chemicals in your eyes, oral cavity, open wounds, or any other orifice.
- The initial investment may be higher than other side hustles. You need to make sure you have

solid equipment and even some backups just in case. For example, you may need two lawn mowers to prevent one from getting worn out.

- Lawn maintenance is not as straightforward as you think. There are a few things you should research or get training for before you attempt them. I also advise you don't do them for the first time in someone else's yard. Stick to what you know.

- Extreme heat exposure when working outside can lead to heat exhaustion and heat stroke, which is a medical emergency. Keep yourself well-hydrated and never go to a job without having enough water with you. If you feel yourself getting too warm, take a break and cool down for a little while.

- Finding clients can be difficult since there are many professionals out there who have been doing it for years.

These are some of the negatives of starting a lawn maintenance side hustle. We will now discuss the pros and hope they entice you into taking on this gig for extra money.

- You will get plenty of fresh air and exercise. It is no secret that lawn care requires a lot of manual labor. This can give you a better workout than going to the gym.

- There are plenty of people who either dislike or don't have time to care for their lawns. If they can find someone else to do it for them, it will make them happy.
- There is a large variety of work you can do. While lawn maintenance is seasonal in many ways, with the wealth of available projects, you can perform it year-round if the weather is at least decent. You can even offer to shovel driveways during the winter.
- The money you bring in is good. People are willing to pay for lawn care as long as the work is performed well. The more jobs you are willing to do, the more money you can make.
- Just like with any other side hustle, you will have a lot of freedom. Eventually, you can create a whole new business out of this side hustle.
- Lawns require a lot of upkeep, so you will get consistent work.

If you are ready to start doing some lawn maintenance work, then let's get going. Remember, you are simply doing this as a side hustle for now. While there are many different jobs you can perform, offer just a few simple ones you know how to do. Determine what those will be and then start gathering supplies needed. A good portion of lawn care is mowing and edging, so it's important to have a good lawn mower and trimmer.

If you plan on using fertilizers or other products on the lawn, learn the proper method for using them and when the best time to place them on the lawn is. For example, fertilizer works best when used during certain times of the year. Figure out what services you will provide and get the proper equipment for it. Take into account things like oil and gas for the mower.

You must also take your own safety into account. Buy high-quality gloves to protect your hands. Also, buy sturdy shoes that cannot be penetrated easily and goggles for eye protection. I recommend wearing a mask to prevent inhaling too many chemicals or debris. Avoid using dangerous equipment you are not trained to handle, like chainsaws. Employ whatever safety measures you can; do not shy away from them.

Once you have the supplies and equipment you need, start advertising your availability. Seek out neighbors who seem busy and often let their lawns go from time-to-time. They may need the most help with upkeep. If you know them personally, you can knock on their door. Also, utilize community newsletters and bulletin boards. Look on freelancing websites like thumbtack or Fiverr and use social media. If you go on Craigslist and look for services needed, there are countless people looking for lawn care projects to be completed. You can also make a professional website through Weebly or Wordspace, and flyers to place in designated areas. Do whatever you can to let your services be known in your community.

As long as the weather is in your favor, you can perform lawn care duties throughout the day. Early mornings are an excellent time to start as it will still be slightly cool. Be aware of any noise ordinance rules our neighborhood may have. Do not mow the lawn at 6 a.m. if you are not allowed to before 8 a.m. Only water the lawn during designated hours. Understand these rules and any other scheduling restrictions, and then go from there. Once again, as a side hustle, various tasks can be performed around yours and the client's schedule. Make sure you have enough time to complete a project before starting it. Do not mow half of a lawn in the morning and the rest some other time. Your best bet is to do it on your days off or make sure you have at least a few hours to spare. This way, you can perform the jobs needed and then have time to clean up.

We will now get into the money you can make. Honestly, this depends on the jobs you are willing to perform. You can certainly charge by the actual project, like $30 for mowing the lawn. If you plan on charging an hourly rate, then 30-40 dollars per hour is acceptable. Get ready, because you will be working hard. It will be rewarding though.

Rating's System Summary:

Experience level: Low-Medium. While many jobs do not require experience, certain projects may require training or at least a little bit of research.

Time commitment: Medium-High. Once again, this depends on the project. Expect to be at a house for at least a couple of hours when you're going to do some lawn maintenance.

Pay rate: $$$.

Babysitting

Babysitting is another popular side hustle for high school and college-aged students. With today's crazy work schedules and the fact that both parents need to work in many households, these types of jobs are abundant. If you have time at all during the day, you can use it for babysitting someone's child. You don't have to be a parent to be a good babysitter either. You simply have to love kids and also be very responsible.

Many people think they enjoy being around kids until they are actually around them for an extended period of time. Before you jump into this as a side hustle, I recommend spending some time around children. You may have brothers, sisters, cousins, or friends who have kids. You may also have younger siblings. Assess how you are around them and determine if babysitting is something you are ready to get into. You must have a lot of energy, patience, compassion, and love. Children will bring all of this out of you. Once you are a babysitter, I can almost guarantee you will find someone in your neighborhood who needs one. We will go over a few pros and cons so you can make an informed decision. We will start with the cons first.

- Some children can be quite frustrating and misbehave constantly, no matter what. Their parents are often more difficult to deal with. They may be the reason children display poor behavior. It is certainly not your place or responsibility to tell parents how to raise their kids. If you cannot tolerate the environment, then it's best to just move on. There are plenty of kids who are angels.

- Kids are full of energy and will certainly take a lot out of you. Chasing them around for a couple of hours can be exhausting.

- It is a huge responsibility you are taking on when watching someone else's kids. You must be vigilant at all times.

- Children that you babysit for a long time will eventually grow up. It can be very difficult to say goodbye when they do. If you are lucky, they will keep in touch.

- Kids can get hurt physically and emotionally. This can be a hard sight to see.

We will now get into the pros of babysitting.

- Children can be a lot of fun, and the best part is you get to have them for fun and games and then turn them over to their parents at the end of the day. Be aware, though, that some parents expect you to keep their kids on a strict schedule. In the end, you must follow what the parents want.
- The side hustle comes with flexible hours and you can make your own schedule. Parents can be desperate at times and will take whatever schedule they can get.
- There are not a lot of prerequisites to being a babysitter. That being said, it is advisable to have basic training in CPR, first aid, and the Heimlich maneuver. There are plenty of organizations like the Red Cross, the American Heart Association, and EMS Safety Services that offer various courses. Your local community centers may also offer complimentary classes once in a while.
- You can make a pretty decent side income, especially when you have more than one client.
- You can save on a gym membership because you will get plenty of exercise chasing kids around.
- If you enjoy watching cartoons and children's programming, then you will have an excuse to do so.

- It will help you learn responsibility.

You really won't need any tools or supplies with you, unless you want to bring some games or forms of entertainment for the kids or yourself while they are napping. If you are babysitting at the parent's home, you can generally just use what they have. Make sure it is clear to you what you can use in the house and how much range you will have. There is a good chance parents will ask for a background check and other screenings. It is their children you are looking after.

Since this job is very flexible, the time commitment can be whatever you make it. Try to pick times when most parents need to be at work. Also, you can ask what nights of the week parents will need help because they may want to have a child-free night. Ultimately, the commitment is up to you.

Start approaching parents in your neighborhood, especially the ones you know, about the babysitting service you offer. Also, advertise in community newsletters and bulletin boards. You can create a website or social media page as well. There are numerous websites you can go to that advertise babysitting jobs specifically. These include care.com, seekingsitters.com, or urbansitter.com. If you are trained in things like CPR or first aid, it will make you more marketable.

Once you start getting clients, then you are ready to jump in and get going. You will have a great time getting to help raise a child. Children certainly have a way of bringing out the positive energy in someone. After working with them for a while, you may get a new outlook on life.

Depending on where you live, you can charge anywhere between 12-18 dollars per hour. If you can put in at least 10-15 hours a week, then you can make a pretty good side income. You can certainly charge more, like 20-25 dollars per hour, if you are looking after multiple kids at a time. You may even be able to make a full-time career out of this if you choose.

Rating's System Summary:

Experience level: Low

Time commitment: Low

Pay Rate: $$$

Housesitting

This can be a pretty cool side hustle, especially if your neighbors have some nice houses. This gig is exactly what it sounds like. You will live in and watch over someone's home while they are out of town for whatever reason. You will also keep the home tidy and safe. As a teen, you will likely just stay there for a few hours during the day, unless you set it up where you will sleep there overnight. People often worry about their homes while they are away. Having a reliable house sitter can ease some of their anxiety. Believe it or not, some people actually travel the world and do this as a career. Since you probably still live with your parents, we will stick to your own neighborhood for now.

Honestly, there is very little experience you need here. You just need to be reliable, trustworthy, and responsible. Before you take on a gig, make sure it is clear what your responsibilities are. Will you simply monitor the home, or will you also be cleaning, working in the yard, taking care of pets, etc. Be very clear about what the expectations will be, especially before you negotiate your price. The following are some of the cons of being a house sitter.

- It can be hard to tell what you are walking into, especially with someone else's home.
- You may never truly feel at home, because you will be in someone else's home.
- Maintenance and repairs on a home can become your responsibility to get fixed while the owners are away. You won't be financially responsible, of course. You will just need to set up appointments and take care of the logistics.
- It may seem like two or three side hustles in one if you are also cleaning the yard and taking care of pets.
- If you damage the home in any way, you will be responsible.

There are many pros to being a house sitter.

- You can live in luxurious homes for free and even get paid for it.
- If you are in college, this is a great way to live rent-free without moving in with your parents.
- There is really no upfront cost as you will simply be living in someone else's home for a while.
- You get experience taking care of someone's home, which will build responsibility for your own home someday. Basically, you learn to be a homeowner.
- You can focus your attention on various projects and not have to worry about paying rent and various other bills.

If you are responsible, clean, and want to save money while also doing a great service for someone, then house sitting is right up your alley. Imagine not only living in a house for free, but actually getting paid to do so. Once again, discuss with the homeowners exactly what your arrangement will be. Will they need you to be a live-in house sitter while they are gone or just take care of the house a few hours a day.

Time commitment can be whatever you decide it to be. This will all be arranged between you and the client. You may be needed for a few hours each day, 24/7 for a short while, or even as a permanent house sitter until you or the client decide to move on. If clients own multiple homes, they may need you to stay in one on a permanent basis and simply take care of their property.

According to housesitter.com, most house sitters charge between 25-45 dollars per hour. Some simply don't get paid and live rent-free with food options. Decide what is best for you and negotiate your price. This is a great side gig and the best financial benefit you will get here is saving a lot of money.

If you are ready to become a house sitter, then begin reaching out to people in your neighborhood. Start small and offer to take care of peoples' homes when they are at work, or even on vacation. If you are aware of someone in your neighborhood who is having trouble keeping up their home due to travel, a busy schedule, or any other reason, then offer to take care of small projects or simply live in the house while they are away. Approaching someone upfront about this may seem awkward. People may think it's weird for someone to randomly come up to them and ask to stay in their home.

To avoid the awkwardness, post about your services online, through community newsletters or bulletin boards, and through various sites dedicated to house sitting. Housesitter.com may be a good option to get your name out there. Going through these dedicated sites can also help to keep you safe by hooking you up with reliable people. Your clients will have some peace of mind too. A background check may be needed before you begin. Once you find clients, you are ready to start.

Rating's System Summary:

Experience Level: Low

Time Commitment: Medium to high, depending if you are a live-in house sitter or not.

Pay Rate: $$

I tried to provide a good overview of what a side hustle is and how you can find them in your neighborhood. There is so much more I can go over. However, I have provided you the information you need to get started. Your own community is full of jobs and once you seek them out, they will become abundant.

If you are still confused after going through all of these side hustle options, don't worry. If none of these tickle your fancy, there are many others out there. Go online and search for people who are looking for help with something. You can find people who need help moving, someone to house sit, a personal driver, and many other tasks almost anybody can do. Get creative and start searching your community for work. You are bound to find something.

Chapter 2:

Offer Your Skills

My hope is that you have some ideas for work you can find near your home. These are quick ways to start making some money. If you are not interested in what we went over in chapter one, or if you want additional work ideas, then there's no need to limit yourself. One of the great things about side hustles is that they are in abundance once you know how to look for them.

The choices from chapter one require a lot of manual labor and not too many special skills besides a good work ethic. If manual labor is not your thing, there are certainly more options to consider. Of course, manual labor can bring you a lot of joy if you give it a chance. But I digress. In this chapter, we will talk about the special skills you possess and how you can use them to make extra money. Over the years, you have probably learned a few things from either life experience or lessons you have taken.

Think about the various skills you have acquired. Have you been playing the guitar for a while? Are you a great writer? Have you studied martial arts? Do you have artistic skills? Are you a math wiz? Assess yourself and determine what skills you have that you can offer to someone else. Once you do this, the next step will be learning how to offer them. We will go over that. You do not have to be a master at what you are offering. You just have to be good enough to make people want to hire you. If you plan on teaching something, just make sure you know significantly more than the people you are teaching.

I will go over a few special skills that many high school and college students possess to help give you ideas. This will provide you with the foundation you need to determine your own skills. Take something into consideration. If you are 18 years old and not very good at math, you may still be able to tutor this subject because you will know far more than a 12-year-old, unless that kid is a genius.

Money Making Ideas

I will go over five money-making ideas in this section that you can start offering if you have these particular skills. If you don't, then you can at least get some ideas for coming up with your own and marketing them to the public. When you start doing the research, it is pretty amazing the various tasks that people need help with. While offering these skills as a side hustle, you will have the opportunity to hone them and gain even more clients in the future. As you get more experience, your wages can also go up. Here are just a few examples of skills you can offer to give you some ideas.

Graphic Designer

Many people think graphic design simply has to do with art. If they are great at art, they will be great at graphic design. While this is a large portion of it, there is much more involved. Graphic design is defined as the practice of planning and projecting ideas and experiences with visual and textual content. Basically, it portrays ideas and messages in a certain way. For example, business logos, posters with complicated designs, book covers, mobile apps, and websites, are all part of graphic design.

There are many things around us that we take for granted, not realizing the thought that went into them. For example, there may be specific designs on a building that catches peoples' attention, but they do not know why. There are certain logos and designs that are so familiar that people would recognize them from miles away. They may even see a small section of a logo and immediately know what it is.

The field of graphic design is very complex and utilizes all aspects of the brain. Color, form, texture, shape, and size are all elements of design. An average person may see a structure and think it was put together haphazardly; however, much thought and effort was likely put into designing it a certain way. If you are a graphic designer, then you know the skill it takes. If you are not a graphic designer yet, then it may be a skill you want to develop. If you are artistic, creative, and don't mind working hard, then this may be right up your alley.

Before you can start offering this skill to other people, you must have outstanding graphic design and photo editing skills. You must be able to see things in a certain way that other people can't. This gives you the ability to make designs that stand out. Before you can start on your own, you will also need an up-to-date computer as well as good software for graphic designs and photo editing. Adobe Photoshop is a great software for doing this.

Your ideal customers will likely be business owners and entrepreneurs. They often need various designs and logos for multiple things like websites, storefronts, flyers, and business cards. A person starting up a t-shirt business could certainly use your help. Your designs could make a real difference. Even non-business owners may need help with certain logos, and you could certainly be there to help them.

You will have a blast working as a graphic designer. Before you get started, you will need training, which can be through various courses online, at a college, or through a specific training program. Before becoming a freelancer, you will need some experience and be able to showcase a portfolio of your work. This way, potential customers will take you seriously. There are many pros and cons to consider before you take the leap. We will start with the cons.

- Your work will be subject to scrutiny. No matter what you think of your own work, what the public decides is ultimately what brings you prosperity. If people don't like your work, then you won't make an income.
- Editing can wear you out and not be worth the original price you quoted. Be clear from the beginning how many edits will be offered and let them know that anything beyond this will come with an extra price.
- It is much harder than people think. Your clients may not realize how long it takes to create great designs, so it is essential to educate them.
- People will not want to pay you what you are worth. This goes back to not thinking your job is that difficult. You must stand your ground about the price because you do not want to be taken advantage of.
- The market is quite competitive, especially in larger urban areas. Of course, the demand will also be higher. Do not discount the rural areas though.
- The work can become tedious, especially with edits.

We will now discuss the pros of this career path.

- Your work will be noticed by a lot of people because many people are visual. Your designs will stick out.
- You get to use the creative and analytical sides of your brain. While you are coming up with creative ways to shape your logos, you will also deal with various measurements. Your entire mind will be at work here.
- You will have a lot of freedom in determining when and where you work.
- This is a highly skilled profession, and your skills will be coveted by many different industries. There are businesses of all kinds that are looking for design help.

After reading through the pros and cons, I hope that graphic design is a skill you would like to pick up. If you already possess this skill, then I hope you are ready to make some offers to the public. If you are ready, then create a portfolio of your work. In this day and age, it will likely be online, but you can certainly have some physical copies of your designs too. Start advertising on freelance sites like Fiverr, Upwork, and Thumbtack. These various sites have different levels of fees, so be aware of those as well, because they can cut into your profits. Finally, as you get clients, be very clear about expectations on both sides, so nobody gets fooled or taken advantage of.

As far as pay, it really depends on the work and where you live. Most graphic designers can charge anywhere from 25-50 dollars per hour. The time commitment will vary too, depending on the actual work. One job may only take you a few minutes, while others will take you several weeks. Graphic design is a great skill to have and your services will be needed by a lot of people.

Rating's System Summary:

Experience level: High

Time commitment: Medium to high, depending on the work.

Pay rate: $$$

Tutor

Tutoring is not necessarily teaching, but more so reinforcing and clarifying what has already been taught. Many students will fall by the wayside in class, because they cannot keep up with other kids. They learn about a subject in class, but a lot of it goes right over their head. They go home and review the teachings, but it does little to help them. This is where tutors come in and save the day. The goal of working as a tutor is to explain and break down various subjects or topics to make them understandable for their students. Tutors usually work in one-on-one or small group sessions.

If you are someone who enjoys explaining and breaking down things for people to make them more understandable, then tutoring may be right up your alley. You can become a tutor for almost any subject and also at any level. As long as you have a good grasp of the subject, are very patient, and are able to explain things in a very simplistic form, then you have a high chance of being successful. You must also realize that there is no cookie-cutter approach to tutoring. Each individual learns differently, and you must be able to adapt your approach when dealing with each person. You will become better at this through experience.

Even if you are not a whiz in the subject matter, you can still tutor people at a certain level. For example, if you are taking a high-level math class like calculus and struggling, you can still tutor lower-level math classes. There are many students in high school and college who need tutors. A more significant percentage of them are also self-conscious and would enjoy smaller group settings or even private tutoring.

There are many students from different levels of schooling who are looking for help. You can advertise your services through various channels and schools that allow you to do so. You can also search through multiple sites like Thumbtack or Craigslist to find people who need help in various subjects. Also, advertise on social media. You never know when one of your friends or followers will need a tutor.

While much of being a great tutor comes from experience, there are courses you can take that teach you how to explain and simplify different subjects. High schools and colleges offer tutoring programs, so you can try to become associated with those to practice and hone your skills. After this, you can start offering your skills as a tutor to those who need it. Consider some of the pros and cons of being a tutor. We will start with the cons.

- It can take a while to get going, just like with any other venture.
- You will not get through to everybody. No matter how good you are, there will be students who you do not click with. They will not learn from your various styles. As a tutor, this can be hard to take because your goal will be to help students learn.
- Some students will try your patience constantly. Unmotivated people can be difficult to deal with.

We will now go over the pros of tutoring.

- You will be making a big difference in people's lives. Many students would fail if they did not receive personalized attention from a tutor. You may help them achieve their academic goals, and that will be a great feeling.
- The demand for tutors is very high. Therefore, this side hustle can be quite lucrative.

- You get to be your own boss and set up a flexible schedule.
- There are very little upfront costs. In fact, besides a couple of basic office supplies, there will really be none.
- You will develop some wonderful relationships with people.
- If you are knowledgeable in multiple subjects, then you can tutor multiple subjects. This increases your income potential.

The time commitment is really up to you. A session is generally about one hour, but with private or small group tutoring, you can customize this. To make a decent income, tutoring about 10-15 hours per week is ideal and definitely doable. The great thing is, you can fit these sessions anywhere throughout the day. If you have an hour in the afternoon between class, you can do a short tutoring session and make some extra cash. You can meet someone at their home early in the morning or late in the evening. The schedule is very flexible.

As a tutor, you can charge between 20-40 dollars per hour. Tutoring a small child in elementary school may not be as intensive as far as the subject matter. For these students, you can charge a little less. If you are tutoring high-level college courses, then you can certainly charge more. Some tutors even have rates as high as 50-60 dollars per hour. You can make a great side income by offering your skills as a tutor and will have a great time doing so.

Rating's System Summary:

Experience level: Medium to high, depending on the subject matter.

Time commitment: Medium

Pay rate: $$$

Music Instructor

Have you always had a talent for music? Are you able to play an instrument, or multiple instruments, very well? Then you can make some great money by offering up your skills. You can perform in front of a crowd and make some extra money. However, there is another way. If you are a talented musician and also love to teach, then consider becoming a music instructor.

You may have heard of people giving private piano or guitar lessons. You can do this as well and make some extra money. Besides being an expert in the musical instrument you want to teach, you will also need to display patience and have the ability to explain things very well. Remember, other people may not have the musical talent that you do, especially at the beginning. You must be able to come down to the beginner level and provide clear instructions.

As far as experience, you should be very well versed in the instruments you will be instructing on, and also be aware of various teaching methods. If you have experience as a teacher or instructor in any field, this will be a big plus. You will also need to know about reading musical notes and how to translate them to the instrument.

There are plenty of people out there that want to learn a musical instrument for school, a career, or just a hobby. Many busy professional and creative souls alike love music. They will love it even more when they learn to create it. You can choose to focus your attention on a specific group of people, like high school kids, or expand to include anybody. To keep yourself from getting overwhelmed at first, you may want to focus on a small group of people.

The only tools you will really need are the specific instruments you will be teaching and any guide books that can help you with the process. Your students should have their own instruments. Before you go any further, let's discuss some of the pros and cons of being a music instructor. We will start with the cons.

- Difficult students and parents can be hard to deal with. Sometimes, it gets easier once you become used to each other. If not, it may be time to move on and find other students.
- Many times, students are not learning an instrument because they want to, but because

they have to. This can cause them to be unmotivated.

- Teaching music can be more challenging than people think and just because you are talented does not mean you can teach it well to others.
- Students will need to practice on their own beyond just your instruction hours. Many of them choose not to.

We will now discuss some of the pros.

- You will get to teach people something you are passionate about.
- As you instruct others, you will build your own skills too.
- You will develop a strong relationship with your students.
- If you are talented in more than one instrument, then you can teach more students.
- You can set up a very flexible schedule.
- Teaching others is very fulfilling, especially something they can enjoy, like music.
- Despite some of the changes in our time, teachers are still very respected.

Since this will be a side hustle, you can set up your own schedule that will work for your clients as well. A single session is usually about an hour, but you can determine that on your own too. If you can put in about 10-15 hours per week, it can provide you a pretty good side income. The average rate from a private music instructor is between 20-40 dollars per hour. You can negotiate the rate with your client and don't be afraid to ask for what you are worth.

The best way to get clients is to reach out to your local community through bulletin boards and newsletters, advertise to local schools and colleges that will allow you to. Go on social media and various freelance sites to search for people looking for lessons, and also advertise through video recordings. For the last one, record yourself playing an instrument and then post it on various sites with an ad stating you are giving lessons. You can even offer complimentary lessons to entice people. Once you start getting clients, you are ready to roll.

Rating's System Summary:

Experience level: High. You must understand your musical instrument well.

Time commitment: Medium. You make your schedule.

Pay rate: $$$

CPR Instructor

Cardiopulmonary resuscitation (CPR) is a valuable and life-saving skill to have that does not, and should not, be exclusive to healthcare providers. The more people that know CPR, the more potential lives will be saved. This is where you come in. Just like you don't need to work in healthcare to learn CPR, you do not need to be in it to teach CPR either. You just have to be knowledgeable about the subject matter and have a love for teaching.

Before you can begin, you must be certified in CPR and then receive your certification as an instructor. There are many different organizations like the American Heart Association, Red Cross, Or National Safety Council that you can become certified through. If you become certified through all of them, then your income potential will increase. Certifications usually stay good for about two years. There is really no experience required beyond this.

Once you acquire the appropriate certifications, then you need to buy some equipment. This includes manikins, an Automated External Defibrillator Trainer, masks, shields, barrier devices, etc. There are definitely expensive models that you can invest in, but they will run you thousands of dollars. You can buy less expensive equipment that will run you less than a thousand dollars and it will still be effective. Another option you have here is to work through a specific company or training center as an independent contractor. In this case, you usually do not have to buy your own equipment and can just use theirs. Your income potential may be lower though. Decide which one is better for you.

Once you have the certifications and equipment, you can begin looking for students. If you work through a training center, they will set up classes for you. If you work for yourself, then you can utilize various online forums to find clients. Many healthcare professional schools, like nursing schools, physical therapy schools, and medical schools have students who need to be certified. Advertise there if they allow you to. Of course, you do not have to be exclusive to healthcare providers. There are plenty of people in the community who want to learn CPR. The more people that have this skill, the better. Utilize freelance sites like Fiverr, Thumbtack, or Lessons.com. You can also make yourselves available to schools, corporate offices, and community centers.

Before you move any further, consider some of the pros and cons of this side hustle. We will start with the cons.

- While the upfront costs are relatively low, they may still be higher than many other side hustles.
- There are extra training and certifications involved.
- Lugging around the equipment can be tiresome.
- Extensive cleaning and disinfecting measures for the equipment are needed before and after every class.
- Students can sometimes be difficult.
- It can often become monotonous as you will be teaching the same stuff over and over again.

We will now look at the pros:

- Teaching can be fun and you can get very creative with it.
- You are teaching people a very valuable and life-saving skill.
- You can earn a pretty good income from this side hustle.
- Classes sizes are small due to teacher-to-student ratio guidelines. This means you can give more individualized attention.
- You will be working for established governing organizations that will provide you all of the knowledge you will need.

After considering these pros and cons, if you are still interested, then let's get going. Each class is usually about three hours long. With set up and teardown time, you are looking at about four hours. You can easily teach two classes a day if nothing else is going on. Be mindful of the ratios. One instructor usually cannot teach more than three students at a time. If there are more in a group, then you can ask another instructor to join you. The average salary for a CPR instructor is 30-50 dollars an hour. Some even charge per student. For example, if they have three students, they will charge 50 dollars each and make 150 dollars. Not a bad way to earn some extra income.

As far as setting up a class, you can do it at an individual's home, your home, or a designated space that you rent out. The space you use must easily fit the instructor, students, and manikins. Arrive about 30-60 minutes before class for setting up and expect to stay for 30 minutes after for clean up and questions. Once you get rolling, you will have a great time as an instructor.

Rating's System Summary:

Experience level: Medium

Time commitment: High as there will be significant preparation time.

Pay rate: $$$

Freelance Writer

Freelance writing is another service you can offer that will provide a nice side income. You can offer your services as a resume writer, ghostwriter, content writer, copywriter, or general freelance writer. Many people are looking for talented individuals to help them with their writing projects and if you have a knack for this, this gig may be right up your alley.

You do not have to be Ernest Hemingway to take on this side hustle. You do have to have a way with words, display proper grammar skills, spelling, and clarity. You should also display a little bit of uniqueness in your writing, because being a robot that can just regurgitate something like anyone else won't earn you many points.

The formality of the writing really depends on the project. With resumes or educational articles, you will certainly need more structure. If you are writing a personal book for someone, then you may have more leeway with creativity. It really depends on the client and what they expect.

If you love to write and feel like you are good at it, then consider this as a new gig to take on. There isn't any formal training involved, but whatever writing experience you have from school or anything else is a plus. I advise that you have a portfolio of writing samples to share as well. You should be knowledgeable about things like APA style formatting and citations. Also, you need to be familiar with various programs like Word or Google Docs. If you plan on becoming a freelance writer through a particular company, then you will have to familiarize yourself with their platform.

Many people out there either do not trust their writing skills or don't have time to create the masterpiece they want. This is where freelance writers come in. You can help someone write a resume to get their next job, you can create content for someone's website, you can write articles and blogs for various organizations, or you can ghostwrite a person's book for them. These are just a few examples, and the opportunities here are endless.

The only tools you really need are a computer and whatever programs are required to create your content. An editing tool to make sure your writing is clear and free from errors is essential. It is hard for one person to catch everything. A second eye is always needed. Once you are ready to get started, search for people on platforms like Fiverr, Thumbtack, and Upwork. You can find people looking for private help on these sites or various writing companies hiring freelance writers.

Freelance writing is a great side hustle that you can literally do anywhere, as long as you have your computer or tablet. There are a few pros and cons to consider. We will start with the cons first.

- Editing can take a lot of time, especially when the client keeps sending the document back for revisions. If you are working with private clients, be clear about how many edits come with the price tag.
- Once people know you are a writer, they will ask you to write small things for them here and there and try to get it done for free. This is common with friends and family. While it is okay to give a helping hand to a loved one, remember that you are running a business and it's okay to be compensated for your work.
- You will be sitting for long periods of time, which can affect your back, posture, and decrease blood flow. Make sure to get up and walk around throughout the day. Also, keep yourself nourished and hydrated.
- The hours can be quite long for each project, especially when it comes to proofreading and editing.

- It is easy to get distracted, especially if you are at home. Limit distractions as much as possible and find somewhere solitary to write. Go to a cafe or library if you need to.

We will now go over the pros.

- Freelance writing can be done literally from anywhere, as long as you have a good internet connection. If you are out of town and want to make a few extra bucks, then see what is available for you.
- Writing is an art form, and you can get very creative with your words.
- The work is plentiful. You may even have friends or family who need something written for them.
- You will meet some great clients.
- You will be able to hone your writing skills with each project. There is always room to grow.
- You can set up your own hours and work whenever you have time.

Depending on the writing project, you could spend anywhere from a few minutes to several days or weeks on a single project. Obviously, a book with extensive research will take much longer than a blog post. Again, the time flexibility comes in great here because you can sit down to write whenever you have a free moment. If you are writing for private clients, you can charge per project, but the general rate is between 20-30 an hour. Hourly rates may be a better option because some projects are more intensive than others.

Once you are ready to get started, begin marketing yourself through various sites, including the platforms we discussed earlier. Create a website or social media page dedicated to your business. Have some writing samples up for potential clients to look at. Be clear about the services you offer and know what your strengths are. Once you start getting clients, set up a schedule and determine what deadlines they need. Don't miss these deadlines because your clients will rely on you. You will have a great time being a freelance writer and will make a great side income.

Rating's System Summary:

Experience level: Medium

Time commitment: Medium to high, depending on projects.

Pay rate: $$$

Do not stop here. These are just a few examples of services you can offer. If there are other skills that you have, consider how you can offer them to the public to make some extra money. You probably have many talents that the public will benefit from.

Chapter 3:

Be Employed

Side hustles are certainly a great way to make money that provides a lot of flexibility. Many people, including teens, are turned off by the instability that it brings. Even the side hustle work is plentiful, searching and advertising can become quite exhausting and time-consuming in itself. Also, you are not guaranteed a stable income like you would with a job. If finding side hustle is not your forte, then there is still the option of being employed part-time through a company. We will go over some employment options that are suitable for teenagers.

Bear in mind that there will be disadvantages to employment over creating a side hustle. The main one will be less independence and flexibility. You will have less busy work to deal with though, like marketing or setting up payment plans. We will go over these in a later chapter.

Employment Opportunities

There are plenty of employment opportunities for teenagers. Several companies around town are looking for young helpers to keep their businesses running. This employment can be part-time, full-time, temporary, or seasonal. Whatever job you can get, it will be a great way to get your feet wet and get experience in the workforce. We will go over some different jobs that are suitable for teens.

Fast Food Worker

This is a very common area for teenagers in high school and college to work. If you enjoy being around people, doing customer service, working around food, and have a lot of patience, then this may be the job for you. There will be a lot of responsibility involved and keeping things sanitary is a must. People are trusting you with making their food. There are no prerequisite skills involved and you will learn what you need to know on the job. The main thing to consider is your personality and how you approach the job.

Eventually, you will need to get quick with the cash register, be able to multitask, stand on your feet for long periods of time, and cook food quickly and sanitarily. If you do a great job, you could be promoted to manager and then have extra responsibilities. At first, though, this will be an entry-level position.

There are numerous fast-food chains you can work at, so do your research and determine which one you like best. Many people who have worked at restaurants claim they started disliking their food because they were always around. Perhaps you should avoid restaurants where you like the food the most then.

Once you get hired, you will simply need the company uniform and a great attitude. I advise that you get comfortable shoes. Working in fast food is a great way to enter the workforce as you will become experienced in many things. Here are some pros and cons to consider before jumping in. We will start with the cons first.

- You will be on your feet all day.
- You will deal with rude customers.
- You may have conflicts with coworkers.
- The job may get boring after doing the same routine over and over again.
- There won't be tips.
- You may get sick of the food and never want to eat it again because you are always around it.

We will now go over the pros.

- You will have great work experience.
- You can learn skills that you can carry for a lifetime, like time management and handling money.

- Shifts can be flexible, which is great for people going to school.
- You can make friends at work that you may not have known through school.
- There is a very high chance of getting promoted. Be aware of the schedule and whether you will have time to take on extra responsibility.

Consider these pros and cons and determine if this is the right job for you. Overall, fast food work is something positive you can put on your resume and a good way for a young person to start earning money. The time commitment really depends on your employer's needs, but expect to work at least 20 hours a week if you are part-time employed. Since the schedules are usually flexible, you can work weekends, after school, or early in the morning, depending on their needs and what works best for you. There are several options when it comes to fast food places to work at.

The hourly rate for an entry-level fast-food job depends on the location. The salary you receive in a major metropolitan area will be different from a small rural town. Research the minimum wage in your location. In some places, it is $7.25/hour; in others, it is $15/hour. The pay can also depend on the company. The current average is about $11/hour.

If you are ready to get started, then begin filling out your application. Since this will be an entry-level job, you will not be required to have previous experience. However, consider the particular skills you have based on your experience and write it down. There are many online job search sites that you can use. If places still allow paper applications, consider going into a location and get face to face interaction. Look out for help wanted signs. These restaurants may be ready to hire you on the spot.

Do not get frazzled if you don't get the first job you apply for. There are many variables in hiring somebody and do not take it personally if you do not get hired. Keep applying until you get that yes. Once you do, you are ready to get started.

Rating's System Summary:

Experience level: Low

Time commitment: Medium

Pay rate: $$

Lifeguard

Becoming a lifeguard is a great option when you're young. You will have a great job, get plenty of exercise, and have a big responsibility. Your goal here is to keep a watchful eye over everybody in the water and make sure everyone is safe. You will also help prevent unsafe conditions by making sure people don't do anything dangerous. If someone is in trouble, it will be your responsibility to save them, whether they are in the water or anywhere nearby.

The minimum age can be as low as 15 to become a lifeguard, but this depends on the state. You will need to be a superb swimmer while also be able to carry someone with you. You will also need to be in shape overall and have basic CPR and first aid certification. You will need to be able to do some training exercises before getting hired. For example, treading water without using arms for one minute, or retrieving a brick and bringing it to the surface. There is a lot of responsibility and you need to be physically and mentally capable of handling it. Most places will require lifeguard certification as well.

One would think this is a seasonal job. However, there are various indoor and outdoor locations you can work at. Any area that has a large body of water is looking for lifeguards, and many different pools and waterparks are always searching too. There are a myriad of options. You should definitely get a lot of experience before attempting to become a lifeguard at a beach where there will be many currents. This is a great path if you love water and enjoy helping people. Saving someone's life is a huge thrill.

Besides the skills you need, there won't be any other equipment required. Your employer should provide you with things like life jackets or swimming goggles. Of course, you can bring your own too if you feel more comfortable. There are some pros and cons to consider before taking this type of job. We will go over the cons first.

- It is not a job you can just jump into. There will be training involved.
- You will get some major sunburns and deal with harsh weather if outdoors.
- Parents will think you're a babysitter and expect you to watch their kids.
- Sometimes, you have to be the bad person and enforce rules like no running or throwing trash on the ground.
- You are risking your life too when saving someone from the water.

Here are some of the pros.

- It is a rewarding job and you will literally be relied on to save people's lives.
- You get to be near water.
- For the most part, people respect you.
- You will be highly trained in multiple skills.
- You will get plenty of exercise.

Being a lifeguard is an exceptional career path you can follow for the rest of your life. The field is really on the same level as other medical professions. The work will be plentiful and you should be able to work whatever hours you can offer, considering the times that the pools, beaches, and waterparks will be open. If you are in school, make sure the company is able to work around your schedule and try to give them whatever hours you can.

The average lifeguard rate is about 9-10 dollars per hour. If you are ready to get started, then obtain all of the certifications and training you need. You can usually get them through various training centers, the American Red Cross, or a community college. There are numerous online career sites, like Indeed, that have lifeguard jobs available. You can also visit specific locations and see if they're hiring. Look for places that are constantly busy and try figuring out the best times to apply, like in the summer. Being a lifeguard can be an excellent job for you while in school.

Rating's System Summary:

Experience level: Medium

Time commitment: Medium

Pay Rate: $$

Golf Caddy

Being a golf caddy is an often overlooked job, but it is a great option for high school and college students. Junior caddies can actually start as young as 14. The job involves carrying the bags of a golfer, cleaning the clubs as you make rounds, and assisting the golfer you're assigned to as needed. All of these activities will be of great help to a golfer.

This job is ideal for a young adult with an athletic build and someone who does not mind some heavy lifting. If you enjoy being outdoors and are a morning person, that makes it even better. There is no real experience or training needed. Whatever tools you need should be available at the golf course. However, you should have basic knowledge of golf and what your responsibilities as a caddy will be. Develop a good relationship with the golfers you'll be working with.

Before jumping into this career, consider some of the pros and cons. We will start with the cons first.

- You will be waking up early. Most golfers like to play in the morning before it gets too hot.
- The golfer you work with may not be the kindest.
- You will be doing a lot of heavy lifting.
- You are essential to a golfer's game but get very little credit.
- It can get very hot at times and the sun will be scorching. Keep yourself hydrated.
- A game may be canceled due to inclement weather, which means you lose out on wages for that day.

We will now go over some of the pros:

- You will get a lot of fresh air and exercise.

- The time commitment is not that much. You can help with one game in a day and work for four hours.
- Golf is a game that attracts affluent people, so you will make some great tips.
- You will develop some unique relationships and can even start networking a little bit.

Going back to the time commitment, if one game takes about four hours, then you can easily fit in two games in a day. You will probably get the most work opportunities during the weekends. The pay rate is anywhere between $20-30 per hour. The real money though comes in the tips. If you help a golfer improve their game, you will get some nice cash awards.

If you are ready to get started, begin looking online for potential employment. Also, visit various golf courses and country clubs in your area to see if they are hiring. Many locations have summer programs.

Rating's System Summary:

Experience level: Low

Time commitment: low

Pay rate: $$$

Retail

Retail is another great option for high school and college students. These types of jobs include clothing stores, grocery stores, pet shops, vitamin stores, and fashion stores. Furthermore, there are various roles you can play within these establishments, like cashier, sales associate, stocker, janitor, etc. Entry-level jobs do not require experience, tools, or training. Of course, you will need to learn the operations of the business, like working the register, once you start your new role. You will also need good customer service skills.

There are numerous employment opportunities, such as the ones we mentioned above. Try to pick out locations you would enjoy working in. For example, if you like athletics, then check out some sporting goods stores. There are definitely some pros and cons to consider. We will start with the cons:

- Rude customers will come in on occasion.
- You will work weekends and holidays.
- You will usually be working indoors.
- You will often be asked to do multiple jobs, like stock, clean, and work the register.
- The pay is relatively low and there are no tips.

We will now go over the pros of this type of work.

- You will gain many different job skills.
- There are many different retail options for you.
- You will get plenty of exercise.
- You will meet some very interesting people.
- Stores often have discounts for their employees.

- There is a lot of room for growth and promotions.

The great thing about retail is that there are varying shifts, so your hours can be flexible. You can work before and after school, on weekends, or even in between classes if you are in college. Many retail stores are close to schools and colleges, so the commute is very manageable.

The pay rate depends on the area you are living in and the minimum wage of the location. Despite the actual job positions, any entry-level role will pay between $7.25 to $9.00 per hour. There are plenty of opportunities for advancement, though.

If you are ready to get into retail, start looking online, or visit specific locations. Look for help-wanted ads too. Some locations are ready to hire on the spot. You can also pick up extra retail work on a seasonal basis during certain holidays.

Rating's System Summary:

Experience level: Low

Time commitment: Medium

Pay rate: $$

Youth Sports Referee

Being a youth sports referee of any kind can be a blast if you love sports. This job will not be for the lazy or unathletic, though. You will be working your butt off and earn your money. You will also need to acquire some skills. First of all, you will have to know the rules of the game you will be refereeing for. You will need to have a pretty strong personality and know-how to be fair. You will also need to know how to take criticism, because you will make many calls that people do not agree with.

To be a referee for youth sports, you will not need too much experience to start off with. You won't need any tools except for the one provided for you on the job, like uniforms, whistles, and flags. It is better to begin with younger kids and then move up the ladder to high school, where the stakes are higher, later on. You will need to be certified through whatever governing body is in your area. This can be a great job option for teens and young adults because of the flexibility. We will go over some of the pros and cons of this job. We will start with the cons first.

- The athletes can be brutal, and so can their parents. You will take a lot of heat.
- You have to be aware of the rules and be ready to enforce them. People don't take kindly to this, especially when the call is against them or their team.
- You are essential to the game but get very little recognition.

- You have to deal with different coaches and their personalities.
- You will deal with inclement weather for outdoor sporting events.

We will now go over some of the pros.

- You get to watch the action in a game up close.
- You will be moving a lot and getting exercise.
- It is a great way to contribute to the community.
- There will never be a dull moment.
- There are many different sports to choose from.

The time commitment for being a youth sports referee is not that high. A typical game for kids usually lasts one or two hours, so you can easily fit it into your schedule. On your day off or during the weekend, you may be able to referee several different games. The average pay rate is between 12-13 per hour and can also vary by sport.

After obtaining your licenses and certifications, you are now ready to start refereeing. Start reaching out to different leagues and organizations in your area and see where they will need you. Places like the YMCA or different recreational centers are a good place to start.

Rating's System Summary:

Experience level: Medium

Time commitment: Low

Pay rate: $$

These are just some of the examples of employment suitable for high school and college students. You may do your research into other options as well. The income potential here is not as great as it is with side hustles. However, these are still good options to make extra money while in school.

Chapter 4:

Create Something to Sell

For this chapter, we will return to the entrepreneurial spirit. There are several money-making ideas where someone can create something and then sell it. These items can include online tools or physical goods that you would like to have.

Making Useful Items

There are many ideas that teens and young adults can take on and create to make a profit off of. We have been seeing this type of ingenuity for generations now. Young people can be creative when they are given the opportunity, whether it is by opening up a lemonade stand, making art to sell, or creating mobile apps during modern times. When high school and college students go this route, they also develop their marketing and selling skills. This can lead to much success with business down the line. This chapter will go over some ideas to help get your creative juices flowing.

Creating an eBook

You have probably seen countless ads out there about eBooks for one subject or another. It seems like everywhere you look, people are putting out eBooks. They are literally all over the internet and range from just a few pages to hundreds. What you may not realize is that these books are being put out by people just like you. They are not world-renowned authors. They are simply people who are knowledgeable about a subject and want to get the information out to the public.

eBooks are a very cost-effective way to earn money on the side. The best part is, you can publish your work immediately without having to reach out to dozens of publishers and hoping for just one response. Anybody can write eBooks. If you are knowledgeable about a subject and feel like you want people to be educated about it, then this path may be right up your alley. Think about the subjects you are well-versed on. It can literally be anything like cooking, bargain shopping, or fixing bikes. Maybe you have gone fishing for several years and feel like you're an expert in it. Write a book about it. If you notice that a subject needs attention, you can even do some research and put it together in a book.

You do not need to be a New York Times Bestselling author here. Basic grammar and spelling proficiency is good enough. Any customer who is interested in the subject you want to write about is a potential customer. It will be good if you can find one or two niches to focus on and develop a repertoire there. People love to get information from a single place and an eBook is a perfect example.

All you need to get started is a computer. You can use the Amazon platform and follow their guide to create and publish your eBook. You can have your book ready to go within days, or sooner if you are a quick writer. There are several other platforms and templates you can use online as well. We will go over some pros and cons of eBook writing for you to consider. We will start with the cons first.

- You will cover the costs of writing an eBook, which are not that high if you are willing to do your own proofreading, editing, and cover design.
- You are responsible for the marketing efforts. There are many sites, like Book Cave, that can help.
- You have to make sure you are as honest and factual as possible to prevent putting out false and inferior content.
- Some people still neglect the benefits of eBooks.
- Indie authors generally do not get the same respect as experienced authors.

We will now go over some of the pros.

- You will have complete control over your book, like where it is sold and how it will be promoted.
- You pretty much have the final word on everything related to your book.
- You will have plenty of support from other indie authors in the same boat as you.
- You get to keep 100% of your net gain.
- Your book will be available on the market much quicker than it would with a traditional publisher.

The time it takes to write an eBook depends on the content, the research involved, and how long you plan on making the book. Once you get better at writing, the quicker you can finish. Publishing on kindle can take just a few hours, or a couple of days, depending on how long the book takes to be reviewed. English titles are published much quicker.

The average earnings from an eBook are about $1,000 in a year. If you write several and on a regular basis, you can certainly make a decent income, depending on the content and marketing. You may not make great money, but it can become a good side income.

If you are ready to start writing eBooks, find your platform and get going. Find the topic you want to write about and figure everything out from there, like the title and content you want to put in it. Also, consider editing and cover design options. If you don't want to do it yourself, you can find people on platforms like Fiverr for relatively cheap. Remember that an eBook does not have to be the size of a novel. Just make sure you fulfill the intended purpose of the book. Once you finish, congratulate yourself for becoming an author!

Rating's System Summary:

Experience Level: Low to medium

Time Commitment: Medium, depending on how often you want to write.

Pay: $

Online Courses

Many entrepreneurial types sell online courses as an extra revenue source. There are several individuals, companies, and educational institutions alike who are going the online course route because it can save so much time and energy in other ways. If you are someone who has a great idea, passion, skill, or knowledge that you want other people to see and learn from, then creating an online course is definitely for you. It is such an excellent way of disbursing information. With the availability of the internet globally nowadays, imagine how many people you can influence.

If you can offer a solution to a problem, then you can likely create a popular online course. You can generate extra income while also providing a great service. Even if you are young, you will have some wisdom to bestow. So, do not sell yourself short. There are plenty of people around the world who will benefit from your teachings, so start creating your online course content. If you have heard of a problem that people are having difficulty solving, then focus on that and create an audience of eLearners. For example, as a younger person, you will have far more knowledge about technology. One idea is to create a course teaching people how to use their smartphones.

Obviously, you will need a computer. Beyond that, having strong knowledge in whatever you will be teaching is a must. You will also need a strong online presence, social network, and email list. Finally, you will need to get on a platform to create your content and do some marketing. The more people that know about you the better. If you have this already, it's a huge plus; otherwise, you can build it along the way. You will definitely spend more time marketing and networking than you will actually creating a course. We will go over some pros and cons to creating an online course. We will start with the cons first.

- You may create something that nobody cares about. It can be hard to gauge what people want and this may cause you to create a course that gets zero traction. Do your research ahead of time and follow trends. Also, try to figure out the most significant problems people are dealing with and come up with content.

- You need to really build up your audience and that can take a long time.
- The eLearning market is getting pretty saturated, but there is still quite a demand.

We will now go over the pros.

- The technology used to be pretty extensive, but now you can use various sites that will set up a sales page for you and even allow you to host your videos all for one low price.
- You own 100% of the content you create and also keep 100% of the profits after some initial investments.
- The courses do not have to be that long to be profitable.
- You will be able to teach and influence many people. Imagine someone from the other part of the world benefiting from your teachings.

The time commitment here varies tremendously based on how extensive and long the course will be. It can take anywhere from 20 hours to hundreds of hours. In addition, you will be doing a lot of marketing to make the public aware of the course. The money you will make is also dependent on how much you can sell the course for and how many people will buy it. At first, you will probably just make enough to have a nice side income. As you improve and sell more courses, you could potentially sell thousands of dollars' worth of courses every month.

Once you are ready to start, decide on your specific course topic based on what you think the public wants. Do the appropriate research that is needed and then outline the course. This includes setting up your goals and objectives and then creating the content. You can then determine your price and begin setting up the course online. After this, it all comes down to your marketing. Additionally, you can begin marketing and building up your audience ahead of time. After your course is entirely available, the income you make will all be passive.

Rating's System Summary:

Experience level: Medium

Time commitment: High

Pay rate: $

Building an App

There seems to be an app for just about anything nowadays. If you can think of it, you can probably search for it in the app store. Many of these apps are created by everyday people who have a great idea. You can build an app for companies to use or mobile apps that can be sold on the app store. People from all walks of life use an app of some sort.

If you are interested in technology and love the major advancements we have gone through, then this is something you can create. Having coding skills is definitely essential. However, there are plenty of platforms today that allow you to work without having to learn how to code. Still, developing this skill set is beneficial. Once you have a great idea, you are ready to go. All you need is a good computer and a platform to help you build apps.

Almost everyone uses an app of some sort. The people who your app will most likely help will be your target audience. Imagine building an app that serves people all over the world. Before we continue, we will go over some pros and cons. We will start with the cons first.

- You have to be technologically sound.
- Building an app can be very time-intensive.
- You may make a lot of money, or none at all.

- Your idea may flop.

Here are some of the pros to consider.

- If the app catches on, you can make a lot of income.
- App building platforms make it much easier than before.
- It may help a lot of people and provide a great service.

The main thing about apps is that building them can take a while. Plus, once you build an app, there will be a lot of marketing to get it well known to the general public. Hopefully, after a handful of people know about it, it will catch on like wildfire. The money you make really depends on the specific app and the users.

If this works out well, it can become a real winner for you. When you are ready to get started, there are a few steps to go through to make it happen.

- Determine what the idea for your app will be and then do the market research to determine if it has potential.
- Create mockups and then design the app.
- Build a landing page and then build the app using a good app platform.

- Once you launch the app, begin marketing it. You can even do some marketing ahead of time to get people excited.

- Once the app is out there, listen to your audience. If they have suggestions for improvement, consider them strongly.

Rating's System Summary:

Experience level: Low

Time commitment: High

Pay rate: $

Selling Photography Online

Selling your photography on sites like Shutterstock or Pexels is actually quite easy. It is also free and can be very profitable over time. After uploading your pictures to one of these platforms, you still retain the copyrights to your work and receive a royalty whenever someone downloads them. If you love photography and also want a way to showcase and sell your work, this will be the perfect opportunity for you.

You will need good photography skills so your pictures will catch people's eyes. You will also need a computer and an account with Shutterstock or whatever platform you will be using. Once you have these, then you are good to go.

People are always looking for stock images to use on multiple projects like books, posters, PDFs, PowerPoints, or just their personal collection. You never know when someone may look at one of your pictures and realize that they need it. This is why it is good to always have something available on a stock photography site. We will go over some of the pros and cons to selling your work through these channels. We will start with the cons first.

- You will make very little money for each picture sold. Usually, it's about 25 cents to start and can go up to 33 cents when more pictures are sold through a subscription.
- They have strict requirements for uploading, so your pictures have to be almost perfect.
- To make good money, you will need to upload a large volume of pictures.
- Slow income growth at first.

Here are some of the pros.

- Once you upload your photos, you will receive all passive income.

- The more exposure you get on stock sites, the more money you will make per picture.
- You will learn and perfect your skills through experience.
- You do not spend any time with clients. They just see your work online and can buy it if they choose.

Once you are able to take perfect pictures, then you can start uploading them through your account. This can take a significant amount of time at first, as you are building up your portfolio volume. The money you make will depend on many factors, the main one being how many downloads your picture gets. The good thing here is the more pictures that sell, the more money you will start making with each picture. For example, once you pass the $500 income mark on Shutterstock, your royalty amount will increase.

Remember, once you upload your photos, they will sit there on the platform and make money for you. Create as many different types of pictures that you can so you get the attention of several different people. You can certainly advertise that you have images online through various social media sites or your own website.

Rating's System summary:

Experience level: Medium

Time Commitment: High

Pay rate: $

Selling Baked Goods

A popular way to make some money, whether for personal income or for charity, is to sell baked goods to the public. Everyone enjoys baked goods, whether they are cookies, pies, cakes, bread, or various other types of food.

Before you jump into this, you will need to have some great baking skills and be able to create many different types of baked goods. Depending on your particular state, you may need a food license and specific permits for setting up. Good baking and customer service skills are the main things you need. In addition, once you have these items, you just need your tools for baking, a large table to set up, and some signs. You may want to buy some new baking ware that is up-to-date and provides you with what you need.

Your customers will be the people who love to eat. If you stick to local areas and clientele, take suggestions from them on what to make based on their requests. The more you listen to your customers, the more business you will create. There are some pros and cons of selling baked goods. We will go over the cons first.

- You have to comply with state regulations, which can become daunting.

- You must ensure sanitary conditions at all times.
- Developing a rapport with your community to start earning some business.
- Baking for long hours can become exhausting.

Here are some of the pros.

- If you truly love baking, then you may not mind the long hours.
- You get to make the food you love.
- You get to set up your own hours.
- You will meet some interesting people, and they get to try your delicious food.
- Once you establish a rapport, you can tailor to your customers' needs.

The time commitment can get quite extensive, especially once you start getting requests. It is not just the time selling, but also the time baking and cleaning that you need to take into account. It may serve you well to stick to items that are easier to bake, like cookies or muffins. Selling by yourself, you will not make a ton of money selling baked goods. Expect about $400 a month, which is a good side income for a teenager.

Once you are ready to get started and have all of the items you need, then start marketing what you sell and your specific locations. Put a message out on social media, notifying people where you will be and when. Have signs that are very visible. You can even start taking requests and orders ahead of time online. If your baked goods are tasty, you will have customers lining up in no time.

Rating's System Summary:

Experience level: Low

Time commitment: Medium

Pay rate: $

You probably noticed that the pay rate is not that high here. Do not worry too much about this because most of these job types are for passive income. Plus, as you build your name and brand, you will see your income going up. At the beginning, expect your pay rate to be low, but never quit trying to get your name out there.

Chapter 5:

Trade Anything

Are you a good salesman? You should consider selling as a side hustle. There are many platforms you can use to sell anything, both online and in-person. We will discuss several ideas that you can start engaging in ASAP.

Start Trading With These Methods

The great thing about using these ideas is that you can start selling and trading if you know what sells and have it available to you. You don't have to create anything ahead of time, except for a website or page on a particular platform. Besides that, you are ready to start making a profit much faster than many of the ideas on the previous chapter.

Domain Flipping

Domain flipping entails purchasing domain names from various registrars on the internet and then selling them to someone else for a profit to an interested buyer. This type of work is ideal for entrepreneurs who have a good sense of what domain names and words would be valuable to a buyer and popular with the general public.

You can also research AdWords on Google's Keyword Tool. Search for words with the highest tracking volumes and try to incorporate them naturally into a domain name. This way, you are following the trends of society. Research and marketing is an essential skill to have for this side hustle. Besides that, there is no experience required and all you need is a good computer with a domain portfolio management software. This will help you keep everything easy, organized, and efficient.

With the access people have to domains at the top-level, one would think this practice is no longer profitable. However, you can still make a pretty good chunk of change doing this, especially when helping those who are not as tech-savvy or familiar with what domains are. Also, individuals who are running their businesses, both big and small, may not have time for figuring out websites and domain names that work. They are happy to outsource this type of work, and this is where you will come in. We will go over some pros and cons for this type of work. We will start with the cons first.

- You will have to invest money first into domain names before making a profit.

- There is no guarantee of a return on investment, this is why it is important to research words the best you can.
- You will not be making money to make you independently wealthy, but you can still make a pretty good chunk of change on the side.

Here are some of the pros.

- It is easy to get started once you have the tools.
- You don't need to be a high-level technological wiz.
- Once you buy a domain name, it is yours until you sell it. So, you can use it and test it out at first. This may increase your ability to sell it for more.
- You can set up a domain name without having to build an entire website and also get them for pretty cheap.
- You can sell to big businesses, small businesses, or individuals.

There is not a huge time commitment involved here. You just need to do some research before purchasing a domain name, and then some marketing afterward to sell it. The profit margins vary based on the domain. However, the average profit margin is around $2,000 for domains that are sold. Not a bad return on investment for the time and money that were put in.

Once again, this is not a guarantee, just something to look forward to.

If you are ready to get started, then you can jump right in. Start researching potential domain names that may be valuable in the future. There are numerous registrars like GoDaddy where you can buy domain names. You can purchase them for as low as $10. Imagine buying 10 at this price for $100 and then selling just half of them for about $2,000. Finally, start marketing your domain name on Sedo, which is a domain auction site. Also, NamePros and DNForum are available as great resources for helpful tips and tricks. Domain flipping can become a great gig for you.

Rating's System Summary:

Experience Level: Low

Time commitment: Low

Pay rate: $$$

Garage Sale Flipping

You have probably been seeing garage sales your whole life as you drive around town. Your parents may have had one. Well, you can make a pretty good profit using a technique called garage sale flipping. How does this work? You basically buy items for a heavily discounted price at a garage sale, and then sell it for a large profit on eBay. You would not believe how many valuable things people get rid of at garage sales because they do not need them.

Well, if you are someone with an eye for value and are great at bargain shopping, then this is great for you. However, even if you are not, there are tools you can use that will help you tremendously. You don't have to have any experience, but just be willing to do a little bit of legwork. Your customers will be those who you find on eBay. People have been selling items on eBay for profit for decades now, and it's time for you to jump in as well.

Basically, drive around and look at the items they are selling at a garage sale. You can then do a quick search on eBay to determine how much the item is selling for. Once you find an item at a garage sale that catches your eye, go to eBay and search for that exact item. Scroll down to "sold items" in the filters and you can see what the particular product has been selling for. For example, the particular product may be selling for $10 at the garage sale, and people are buying it for $100 on eBay. People will often sell treasure chests without even realizing it.

All you need is a computer, a smartphone or tablet for when you are out searching, and an eBay account. Also, you must have patience because there will be many garage sales where you find nothing of value. We will go over some pros and cons of garage sale flipping. We will start with the cons first.

- You will need a lot of patience.

- Sometimes, you may need to haggle for a lower price.
- You may find nothing to sell.
- The item you purchase may not sell on eBay.
- You will have to ship items yourself.

Here are some of the pros.

- You can make great profits on single items.
- People at garage sales will often sell vintage items in mint condition.
- eBay has a lot of traffic on their site and it's easy to research.
- You just need one or two big hits a week to make some good money. Imagine buying $100 dollars worth of items, and then just one of them selling for $1,000.
- Expenses to buy items can be written off.

The time commitment for this side hustle can be quite high, especially when you are traveling around looking for garage sales. You may have to wait a while for your item to sell once you place it on eBay.

The profits you make can range from $100 to $1,000 or more. The more you sell, the more you make. So, it's pretty simple in that regard. Here's an extra tip. You do not have to limit your purchases to garage sales. You can bargain shop at many places and you will be floored by some of the things you can purchase at a discounted price.

If you are ready to get started, then gas up your car, and start finding some great deals. Set up an eBay account. You may also advertise your eBay link on social media. The more good reviews you receive on eBay, the more potential customers you will have.

Rating's System Summary:

Experience level: Low

Time commitment: Medium

Pay rate: $$

Dropshipping

This is a new wave of buying and selling products online. Through a dropshipping site, you can sell products to customers at your own price, and you don't even have to carry inventory or pay for it until it is sold. Once you have made a sale on an item, the supplier will ship your products directly from their warehouse. It seems like a win-win for everybody. All you need is the entrepreneurial spirit and knowledge of how items get sold through the various sites.

You do not have to have any experience getting started. Once you get set up, you can start selling your products to interested customers. You can focus on specific items and set up your regular customer base, or you can sell a wide range of supplies to target numerous groups. To get started, all you need is a good computer and then set up an eCommerce platform. Here are some pros and cons to consider when setting up a dropshipping business. We will start with the cons first.

- You will have to do research on finding products that sell.
- You will have to rely on other peoples' stock, so finding a good distributor is essential.
- You don't get the bulk pricing for items you want to sell, so you will likely pay more for each item.
- Even though you do not personally handle the products, you will get the blame from many customers if they arrive damaged.

Here are some of the pros.

- You do not have to handle, package, or ship any products.
- You generally don't have to pay for inventory until it is sold.
- Low Startup costs.
- You can update your inventory quickly and have a diverse number of products without having to worry about storing them somewhere.

Dropshipping is great for people who simply want to play the middleman between the seller and buyer. You will be spending some time setting up your store, selecting products, and deciding a pricing strategy before you start selling. Setting up your store is where the majority of the work is. The money you make depends on the hours you put in and the amount of inventory you sell. Some people make well over a hundred thousand dollars a year, but they are selling thousands of products a month. As a student, selling a couple of dozen a month may be all you can do for the time being.

When you are ready to start a dropshipping business, consider the following steps. This may be easier than you think.

- Come up with a dropshipping idea and products to sell. Some people focus on what their passion is. However, you should also research products that are popular and will make you a profit.
- Perform a competitor analysis to determine what your competitors are selling and for how much. You want to stay competitive in the market.
- Find a good supplier. You can find good suppliers from sites like Oberlo, where you can see the reviews and ratings.
- Build a dropshipping business store by setting up a domain name, building your site, and

signing up for Shopify, which is the most comprehensive eCommerce store around.

- Market your dropshipping business everywhere, including social media.

Dropshipping is a great business model that has benefited a lot of people.

Rating's System Summary:

Experience level: Low

Time commitment: Medium

Pay rate: $$

Flea Market Flipping

Flea Market flipping is a similar concept to Garage Sale flipping. You can buy various products from flea markets, yard sales, or discount stores, and sell them for profit through platforms like eBay, Amazon, Craigslist, or Facebook. If you love bargain shopping and have an entrepreneurial spirit, then consider this great business idea.

You will need to have a lot of patience and the ability to look for sellable items. Also, you'll need a smartphone or tablet to look up prices for items that you find is essential. For example, if you find an old video game in mint condition, research on eBay or Craigslist to see how much the item is selling for. If the profit is worth it to you, then consider buying for a low price and selling it.

You will have several customers through various online platforms whom you can sell to. You can focus on a few products or sell a diverse number of items. You can also do some market research on what people like to buy. All you need to get started is a computer, smartphone, and an account with the websites we mentioned above. Consider some of the pros and cons of flea market flipping. We will start with the cons first.

- You will have to spend a lot of time and effort looking for sellable products.
- Several products you buy may not sell.
- If you don't do your research, you might pay more than you need to.

Here are some of the pros of this business plan.

- You will have a lot of freedom.
- You will meet some interesting people as you go around shopping.
- You can sell through multiple platforms.

The major time commitment comes from going around and shopping for items. Once you have your inventory, then you must post them online. Make sure you take a good photo to put up. You want the product to look good. If you or someone you know is great at taking pics, then that's a plus. Finally, once the product sells, you will have to package and ship it.

Through flea market flipping, you can potentially buy an item for $10 and then sell it for several hundred dollars. Many people create full-time incomes through this model. For now, your goal is to make a little extra money on the side.

Once you are ready to get started, you just have to set up your various accounts and then start shopping and buying. Post the items you want to sell and wait and respond to customers as they become interested. Make sure to market your business on social media and other platforms as well.

Rating's System Summary:

Experience level: Low

Time commitment: Medium

Pay rate: $$

Selling Your Old Items

You may have a treasure chest in your closet. If you love to sell things and feel like you have valuable products in your home, then you can start decluttering and getting rid of some stuff. Clothes that you have outgrown, toys you no longer play with, and books you have already read are some examples of things you can sell. You can also sell your parents and siblings items, but make sure to ask them first.

The old saying, "One person's trash is another person's treasure" is attributed to this business model. Items that you no longer want may be a necessity for someone else. Hence, you will have many potential customers. Never discount anything you have that may be able to get sold. While some products may not have a great resale value, other vintage items may have gone up in price. Check out sites like eBay and Craigslist to find out what various products are selling for.

All you need is a computer and an account with different sites to start selling. There is no experience required besides the research you will need to do. This is a fairly easy thing to set up. We will go over some of the pros and cons of selling your own products. Here are some of the cons to start off with.

- It can be hard to let go of things due to their sentimental value.
- Some products may sell for less than what you bought them for.
- Decluttering can take a while.
- Profits are limited because you can only sell items that are in your home.

Here are some of the pros to consider.

- You will not need to buy inventory since it is already in your house.
- You can collect a lot of money on your old items.
- You will be able to minimize your belongings and make room for more products if desired.
- You will be helping people by providing the items they need.

The time commitment here is much lower than the previous ideas because you will eliminate shopping around. You will still have to post about your items, market, and then ship them.

Just like with garage-sale flipping, you can potentially sell vintage products for several hundred dollars in profit. Once again, research the market through various sites to determine what specific items are selling for.

Once you are ready, collect the items you want to sell and begin uploading them to eBay, Craigslist, Facebook, and other sites that allow you to sell. When posting about an item, make sure to put any flaws they may have so the customers are fully informed.

Rating's System Summary:

Experience level: Low

Time commitment: Low

Pay rate: $$

Learning to sell through various methods is a great way to start making extra income.

Chapter 6:

Earn from Ads

There has been an online revolution going on in the world for several decades at this point. It has never been easier to connect with people around the world through various online channels. Once you are able to understand how this works, you could create content that will attract a large audience, which can eventually lead to earnings from advertisements.

Creating Content to Attract Advertisers

You may have heard of YouTube stars who have posted videos that generate millions of dollars. It sounds like a great gig, right? Well, it may be harder than you think. The concept here is that you are creating content that will attract an audience. If you can attract a significant number of followers, then advertisers will become interested in paying you to be promoted on your sites. Another great thing about these activities is that they can be fun and fuel your creativity. It can certainly take a while to build an audience, so be patient.

Create a YouTube Channel

A lot of people are on YouTube these days. You can find content for just about anything. When you have a YouTube channel, your goal is to create content that will be attractive to people, whether entertaining, educational, dark, or light-hearted. Once a large number of people view your videos, you can attract sponsors who want to display their ads on your channel.

If you are creative and have some great ideas for videos that will catch the public's eye, you may have found the right path for yourself. It is not always as easy as standing there and talking in front of the camera. You must be engaging, have proper light, great content, and be able to tell a story. Finally, you need to have video editing skills so you can upload a professional-looking video.

There is no experience required beyond knowing whatever you will talk about. You must have good editing software, a computer, and a good camera. The camera on your phone is acceptable. You may want a higher quality one later on. Some YouTubers also invest in selfie sticks that rotate on their own to provide better views and angles. If you make great videos, you will attract viewers who are interested in your content. Even if they are not interested in your content, they may just like you as a personality. Consider some of the pros and cons of being a YouTube personality. We will start with the cons first.

- It takes time to build an audience that you can monetize.
- It's a highly competitive market.
- May need to spend additional money to create quality content.
- Some of your content may get demonetized if it does not follow the guidelines of YouTube.
- You may get very few to zero subscribers.
- You need to be over 18 or have parental consent to be on YouTube.

Here are some of the pros.

- Potential for huge passive income. Once you have a large following and sponsors, each video you create could bring in large sums of money.
- Work and create content whenever you want.
- Create content you are passionate about.
- Have the ability to help and influence people around the world.

You may want to choose a niche market to focus on. The time commitment can be high, especially when trying to build an audience. Also, creating, editing, and uploading a video can take a while if you want them to look professional. YouTube requires a minimum of

1,000 subscribers, and 4,000 viewing hours before you can monetize and join the partner program.

The top earners on YouTube make millions of dollars. It will take you some time to get to that level, but keep working for it. Initially, you will just be making a small chunk of change.

You can get started by using the following steps:

- Find a niche or specific content you want to focus on.
- Create a YouTube account. Think of a unique name, icon, and art that goes along with your content.
- Begin making and uploading content and playlists.
- Start sharing your content. Do not rely on YouTube to market you. Post your videos anywhere you can.
- Analyze the data, like which videos are getting the most responses.
- Stay engaged with your audience. Follow the comments and answer questions if you can.

Rating's System Summary:

Experience level: Low

Time Commitment: High

Pay Rate: $; low at first with the potential to become a millionaire.

Creating a Blog

Blogs are websites that focus on written content, like articles or short blurbs. Bloggers often write from a personal perspective. There are numerous types of blogs on just about any type of content. Just like with YouTube, your goal is to create content through writing that will attract followers. Once you have enough followers, then you can bring in sponsors as well. If you are creative, and enjoy writing content of any kind, then blogging is right for you.

You do not need any experience before starting a blog beyond being knowledgeable in whatever content you decide to create. All you need to get started is a computer and a creative writing mind. You can literally write on anything. Some people choose educational posts, while others choose entertaining ones. You can have a combination of all. Search around and see for yourself how many different blog types there are. Consider some of the pros and cons of creating a blog. We will start with the cons first.

- You will have to do a lot of writing before getting noticed.
- You may or may not ever get noticed.
- People will be critical of your work, especially if you have controversial topics.

- It is quite a saturated market, but you can still stand out.

Here are some of the pros to consider.

- You will be able to publish your content immediately.
- You will get to practice your writing skills.
- It's a great medium to express yourself.
- You will find many like-minded people.

The time commitment can be high at first while you are creating your website. After everything is set up, you must write blogs regularly. Being absent can cause your audience to become concerned or disinterested. An article can take around 30 minutes to write, depending on the content and how fast you are.

The highest level bloggers can make hundreds of thousands to even millions of dollars. Article clicks essentially pay you once you have sponsors set up. You can make around $0.01-$0.10 per article click. It will take a while to build up your audience and start getting sponsors.

If you are interested in blogging, here are some steps to get you started:

- Choose a platform to begin blogging. WordPress is the most popular one to use. There are reasons that so many people love this platform, and that's because it provides many benefits. Other options are Blogger or Tumblr.
- You can set up a free blog or pay a fee to create one. If you pay, you will have some advantages,

like owning your domain name. There are different levels of fees, depending on the services you want.

- Design your WordPress page to your liking.
- Start blogging and creating content.

Rating's System Summary:

Experience level: Low

Time commitment: Medium

Pay rate: $

Podcasting

Podcasting has revolutionized the way the spoken word is used. It has even replaced old-school radio and many media outlets as well. People often trust podcasters more than regular journalists these days. There are podcasts for almost any topic you want, and it is easier to start one than ever before. As of June 2020, the market is still not nearly as saturated as blogging. If you are someone who loves talking on-air and has something valuable to share, then podcasting may be the right forum for you.

There is no real skill required. You just have to be able to talk, convey your message, and attract people with your words. This is actually more difficult than it sounds, especially when you are talking to people through various online channels. Your customers will be your listeners, so determine what subjects you want to talk about and what is popular at the moment. Chances are if you like something, many others will too. They just don't know anyone has the same interests.

You don't need a lot of high-tech equipment. In many instances, you just need a phone, computer, and a decent microphone for voice quality. After that, several platforms can be used to create a podcast. Consider some of the pros and cons of podcasting. We will start with the cons first.

- It will take a while to build an audience.
- You will not get to see the reactions people have to your words.
- Talking for long periods can be exhausting and if you don't have enough content, there will be a lot of dead air time.
- You may not have any listeners at all.

Here are some of the pros.

- You can talk about what you love.
- You will be able to interview guests who you enjoy talking to if you do an interview-style show.
- You can get creative and truly discuss almost any topic.
- You will have fewer regulations than other media outlets.

- You can decide the lengths of your shows.
- It's easy to record almost anywhere.

There can be quite a large time commitment for podcasting, especially when it comes to coming up with content, researching, editing, and uploading. Oh yeah, you also have to record content too. Your commitment also depends on how often you do the podcast. Your audience will not enjoy long periods of absence.

Eventually, when you have enough viewers, sponsors will become interested in you and start paying for ads. If you make it big, you can make millions of dollars. Think about the Joe Rogans of this world. Of course, you do not have to become Joe Rogan or Adam Carolla to be successful. You can build a nice audience of a few thousand people and make some decent side money. It will take a while to even get to this point. Remember, your podcast can be available worldwide.

If you are ready to get started, then take the following steps:

- Choose a topic, or topics, that your podcast will cover.
- Consider getting a co-host to bounce things off of.
- Choose a catchy name for your new show.
- Determine the format, including length, style, show introduction, and the closing statements.

- Set up your equipment and choose a podcasting platform, like Podbean or SoundCloud.
- Begin recording your show. Edit the show before uploading through the platform.

You can have a great time doing a podcast and start bringing in some passive income.

Rating's System Summary:

Experience level: Low to medium, depending on how high-tech you want to become.

Time commitment: High. This also depends on the show's length and how often you will record.

Pay: $

Instagram Influencer

Instagram has become an amazing social media website where people can share their pictures for other people to see. You can become an influencer on Instagram once you've established a large audience and credibility. For example, numerous fashion influencers can encourage many people to buy a piece of clothing simply because they are promoting it. It's like when a celebrity wears a dress on the red carpet and the sales spike almost instantly.

If you love Instagram and don't mind documenting aspects of your life on it, then you can also become an Instagram influencer. Once you have a major following and credibility, various brands will swoon over you to help sell their products. You can make a pretty good chunk of change by simply posting great photos of yourself. The top influencers make millions of dollars. It will take a while to get there. For now, any side income you can make will be a blessing. Your customers will be your followers.

There is no real experience required, you just have to be able to influence a large number of people to do something. For example, some influencers can create excitement over a hotel and cause people to want to go there. This can take a while to do, and I will provide a few tips later on. Your best bet is to follow other influencers and figure out their tricks. You must have a computer, an Instagram account, and a good camera. The camera on your phone should work if you know the tricks. There are some pros and cons to consider when becoming an influencer. We will start with the cons first.

- It will take a while to build an audience.
- Your personal life is somewhat on display.
- You must upload the perfect picture.

Here are some of the pros.

- You can make passive income once you become an influencer.
- Many people will trust you.

- You have the potential to reach a lot of people.
- There are many influencers you can follow.
- You can influence people while living a luxurious lifestyle.

You will have to put in a significant amount of time while building your audience. You will always need to be aware of good opportunities to take a good picture. You are essentially always working and influencing people.

To start making money, you will need many followers. As you increase your followers, you will also make more money per post. For example, an influencer with 10,000-100,000 followers can earn about $200 per post. Any more than this, and it can go up to over $600 per post.

If you are ready to become an influencer, then take the following steps:

- Think about what makes you unique and capitalize on it. For example, you may be a great comedian or cook.
- Get rid of your insecurities and don't be shy. You have to let your audience into your life. Of course, there are things you can still keep private.
- Document your life; don't create one. Document many of the things you do regularly through photos.

- Stick to a particular aesthetic so your audience can follow you.
- Invest in a good camera and maybe even photography lessons.
- Make yourself available for sponsorships.

Rating's System Summary:

Experience level: Low

Time commitment: High

Pay rate: $

Affiliate Marketing

Affiliate marketing is the ability to earn commissions by promoting other people's products. If you find a product you like, you can promote it to others and earn a percentage of profits for each sale. There are products you use every day that you can promote. The merchant of the product will give their affiliates a link they can put on their sites. If an individual clicks on the link and purchases a product, they can track the link it went through and give commissions. You can also receive a commission if a buyer delays purchase.

The more followers you have, the more commissions you can make. There is no experience needed. You just need to be familiar with the product since you are putting your name to it. You just need a computer and any type of site where you can post the affiliate links. You can even use your private Facebook page. Your customers will be whoever follows you. Consider some of the pros and cons. We will go over the cons first.

- You have no control over the affiliate markets that exist, so you just have to use the ones there are.
- You don't establish a customer base. A repeating customer usually won't purchase from you again.
- There are no revenue guarantees.
- People may feel like you are spamming them.

Here are some of the pros.
- Low investment costs.
- It's a billion-dollar business.
- There's a lot of convenience and flexibility.
- You don't have to deal with customer service.
- The vendors provide marketing materials, so you don't have to create your own.

You can start making money as an affiliate marketer almost right away. However, the commissions will be low for a while. High-level earners can make over $3,000 in a day. When you start out, you may be making just a few dollars a day and may get up to a few hundred a day if you stick with it.

To become an affiliate marketer, consider the following steps:

- Review products in your niche. Consider the products you use and love.
- Build an email list with your prospects on it. Email is still a great marketing channel.
- Educate your audience with webinars and other educational tools to keep people informed about the products you are affiliated with.

Rating's System Summary:

Experience level: Low

Time commitment: Medium

Pay rate: $

I put a low pay rate on all of these ideas because you will not make a lot of money to start. Once you build your audience, you will have the potential to make a lot of passive income.

Chapter 7:

Getting into the Nitty Gritty of Making Money

Throughout this book, we have gotten into various ways for young students to make money through many different side hustles and forms of employment. Look at the different types of work we have described and determine if any pique your interests. If they don't do that, maybe they will at least open up your mind and give you new ideas. One of the major objectives of this book was to give you a whole new perspective on how to make money that is not traditional. There is a wealth of work out there that will allow you to make more money, so take advantage of this.

Administrative Responsibilities

For this chapter, we will discuss an often overlooked section of side hustling, and those are the administrative responsibilities. It is not just limited to working and making money. There are numerous things you need to take care of behind the scenes to make sure the jobs you take on go smoothly.

The first thing you must do is figure out what jobs and side-hustles will pique your interest. If there are multiple ones that do, then don't be shy about taking on several different ones. Of course, make sure you do not overwhelm yourself. I have no idea what your school schedule is like. Look at it for yourself and determine what hours work best for you and what days of the week are most convenient. Make sure your clients are fully aware of the time commitment you can give them. School needs to remain your priority. The income you make from these types of jobs is simply icing on the cake.

Inexperienced freelancers have a hard time determining what they should charge. My advice is to research the market conditions in your area and what freelancers who are doing similar work also charge. Be aware of the value you bring to the client based on your skill level and experience. Do not shortchange yourself and also do not purposefully try to cheat the client. This will do nobody any favors. Decide for yourself if you want to charge by the hour or per project. Honestly, it depends on the specific type of work to determine which option is better for you. For example, mowing the lawn could be per project, but clearing weeds could be charged by the hour. Just make sure you and the client are both clear about this.

I recommend that you sign an official contract for the work you agree to do. You can find freelance contract templates online that include sections for your name, the client's names, the work to be done, the agreed-upon payment, and other essential terms and conditions. Many freelance platform sites already offer contract services and mediums to communicate with clients. If you are not using a freelance platform, then please make sure a contract is signed. Also, keep track of any written communication through email or texts. This is to protect you and the client. The last thing you want is to deal with legal issues that could have been avoided.

As far as receiving payments, you can certainly go the old-fashioned way by taking cash. Make sure to keep a record of the cash you take in and deposit it immediately for security. We will discuss this more later. Please look into more advanced payment intake methods as there are plenty. For example, you can install a tool that attaches to your phone so that you are able to take credit card payments. There are plenty of credit card apps on the phone too.

PayPal is a popular and secure method of taking payments. Other methods can be CashApp or Square. I advise that you don't set up automatic payments yet and simply charge when you are about to do the work. For projects that will take a long time, like days or weeks, cut it down into payment plans. This way, the client will not be burdened with one huge payment, and you will feel secure knowing that you are getting paid for your work.

Invoices should be maintained for the work you do. You can easily create these online through various sites, including directly on PayPal. Invoice your clients promptly so that you remain up-to-date for the work that you do. This will ensure that you keep good records too. Establish some guidelines on late payments. You can certainly be flexible now and then, but make sure you put in specific deadlines for payments that the clients are aware of. Also, make sure they know about the fees associated with late payments. You have a right to get paid on time. I hope it never gets to this point, but if the client refuses to pay you, you can turn the matter over to a collection agency. This is why it's important to keep good records.

I have mentioned these throughout the book; however, take advantage of freelancing and side hustle platforms like Fiverr, Upwork, Thumbtack, Freelancer, and even Craigslist. Countless job opportunities are available on these sites, and you can even market your own services on them to find potential customers. Creating your own website is also a plus. Social media can be utilized as well and you can create quite a following on these various sites. You can even make a separate business page if you don't want to deal with the social media drama.

I advise you to attend local networking events where people can learn about each other, develop relationships, and recommend each others' businesses. Finally, the old-school methods of word-of-mouth and email are very beneficial. It is hard to believe that email is now an old school method, but it has been around for a while. It is still an effective marketing tool. You want people to talk about the great work you do. Real-life stories help sell products and services.

The hardest thing for new freelancers to do is to negotiate. It can be intimidating, and the thought of losing a client can be difficult to deal with. One thing to remember is that you are offering a valuable service. Charge based on your experience, values, and end results. Your work should speak for itself. It is okay to negotiate down on a price, but always set a minimum rate you are not willing to go below. Neither you nor the client should feel cheated during the transaction. Try to negotiate other things besides just price, such as offering a small extra service for loyal customers. You can even offer discounts for early payments—whatever you can afford to do and still make a profit.

Taxes

Taxes are never a fun thing to think about, and it never becomes something people enjoy doing. It is part of the game though, and you cannot avoid it. Even minors have to pay taxes. You may as well start learning about it early. Whether you work for an hourly wage at a job or perform various side hustles, you will not get to keep everything you make. Until they somehow change the system, this will be a reality.

If you work for an employer, they will have you fill out a W4 and other appropriate tax documents. You will have a certain amount of money withheld from your check every time, which are the taxes being deducted. If you are a minor, your parents could help you fill out the paperwork. During tax season, you will receive a W2 form, and the information needs to be filed with the IRS. From here, the government will determine if you need to pay more, or if you paid too much and will get a refund.

If you are doing unofficial jobs, like the side-hustles we mentioned throughout this book, you will have to keep very good records of all of your earnings and expenses. Certain items that you spend for your business can be tax-deductible, so definitely make sure to keep track of them. In addition, money from investment accounts, gifts, or inheritances all needs to be reported. Basically, if you make any type of money at all, the government wants to know about it. If you are making money through some type of side hustle, remember that taxes are not being held automatically. You must set a good majority of it aside to pay out your taxes later.

If you are under 18, you should discuss filing for taxes with your parents. There are several online programs, but you can also hire a professional. This is something for you to decide, and I will not recommend one way or the other.

Taxes can certainly seem like a burden. Most of us would much rather keep all of the money we make. Educate yourself about the importance of taxes and what they are for. Ask your parents for information too. The roads we drive on, the schools that are built, the post office, and various other programs and services are funded by tax dollars. They are essential to keep the country moving. Once we understand the purpose of taxes, it becomes easier to accept them being taken out of our accounts.

Chapter 8:

What to Do With Your

Money

We have gone over many ways to make money. What's amazing is the variety of ways we can make money from credit devices, mobile apps, PayPal, and various other online platforms. My goal for this book was to get young students more educated about money. This does not just mean bringing more in but also learning to save and helping it grow.

I will not be giving you specific financial advice here. I will be teaching you about the value of money and the importance of not wasting it. It is painful to see so many individuals make countless amounts of money that most people cannot even imagine, only to spend it completely and have nothing to show for the future. Poor financial habits are detrimental, no matter what career path, or paths, you end up choosing. Before you worry about making extra money, focus on managing what you have. Otherwise, no matter how much you make, you will always be broke.

Before we get into specific money management techniques, let's swing back around to the various money-making options we have discussed. You may have noticed that several of them can be done in less time than others while also being very flexible. As you enter into the working world, I want to encourage you to set yourself up so that you have more than one source of income. With the volatile job market we live in, it is difficult to rely on one source of income. Furthermore, there are too many ideas out there for us to ignore. If we neglect taking advantage of so many opportunities, we are doing ourselves a great disservice.

Here is another thing to consider. You can use the various sources of income to fund different areas of your life. For example, you can take the income from one source to put into your savings account and the income from another source to pay bills. Having more than one way to make money will help put you at financial ease.

Saving Money

Here's the bottom line: if you do not learn to save money, you will spend all of it and always end up broke in the end. Your salary and income can continue to increase, but if you don't fix your spending and financial habits, it will not matter in the end. You may get a few thrills and buy some toys along the way. However, this will not matter much when you have to sell things to make some of your money back. I am not telling you not to have fun. You work hard for your money and, of course, you should enjoy it. I am just saying you don't have to spend all of it to be happy. You have to save up for the future.

The first thing we must do is set up a budget. This is where you determine your expenses and income and assess if you are bringing in more money than you spend. If you are not, then you need to make some major shifts in your finances. This means you need to reduce some of your spendings, figure out a way to increase your income, or a little bit of both. Setting up a budget can be tedious. However, it is necessary if you are to manage your finances properly. We will go over the steps to creating a budget. Make sure to write everything down so you can see it visually.

- The first thing you must do is calculate your expenses. Add up all of your expenses every month, whether it be from eating out, monthly bills, insurance, payments, or any other expenses. There are some payments that you may not have to make monthly, like car insurance. This is why I suggest adding up your total expenses for six months to a year and then dividing by the number of months. For example, if your total for six months is $8,000, then divide by six, and you will get your average monthly expense rate of about $1300.

- A good rule of thumb is to calculate what 10-15 percent of your monthly income is and then add it on top to get your total. For example, 10 percent of 1,300 is 130, so your total monthly expenses are $1,430. This strategy will account for any miscellaneous expenses that may have been missed.

- Next, determine what your monthly income is. Calculate all of your income that you may be receiving from jobs, side hustles, allowances, etc. Add all of these income sources together for one month. If your income changes month to month, then you can calculate an average as we did with the expenses. We will say your monthly income average is $1,600.

- Take your total income and subtract your expenses. In this case, 1,600-1,300=300. For our example, we are positive and earning more than what we spend. This is a great start.

- Don't be satisfied here. Look for ways to increase income and reduce expenses so you have more money to put away. If your expenses are greater than your income, this is not good. Make some changes right away. What expenses do you have that can be taken out? What can you do to increase your income?

- Revisit your budget report on a regular basis to make sure you are not falling into the red.

Okay, so you have $300 extra per month, which is good. What will you do from here? Stick it in your piggy bank or under the mattress? That's not a bad idea, but what if the money gets lost? It is better to have it in a secure location. This brings us to the bank and setting up your various accounts to keep our money safe. The great thing about savings and checking accounts is that our money is FDIC insured. This means the bank is liable for giving us back everything we put in.

If you are a minor, then you will need someone to open up an account for you. I encourage you to set up multiple accounts and distribute the money throughout all of them. If you keep all of your money in one account, you are more likely to spend it. If you keep it separated, then it is easier to determine what you spend and what you save. We will discuss three types of accounts you can open.

- A savings account can be used to store money away. This is money that you simply save and don't plan on using unless there is an emergency or big expense. A high-interest account like a money market account is good because it will provide you with high yields over time. Remember that savings accounts are set up for just that: savings. They often penalize you with fees when you take money out. So, do your best not to withdraw if possible.
- A checking account is one where you can easily deposit and withdraw with a check, debit card,

or ATM. Put all of the money that you plan on spending for any reason into this account.

- Certificates of Deposit or CDs are basically accounts that yield relatively high-interest rates. There are many different types of CDs, so it is best to go to the bank and determine which one is best for you. If you can set up an account like this early in life and deposit for several decades without removing anything, then you will save a lot of money throughout your life. A CD is a nice and safe investment account to open.

As you continue to have income coming in, distribute it throughout all of these accounts. You can decide what percentage you put in each based on your personal finances. The more you put into savings between the savings account and CD, the better. Saving money is a powerful tool that your future self will love you for. When you get into the habit of it early, you are more likely to maintain it for the rest of your life.

One more concept I want to go over is the idea of paying yourself first. This simply means that when you bring in any form of income, put aside a certain percentage of it right away before you use the money for anything else. For example, if you get paid $500, immediately save 10 percent of it, which is $50. Too many people forget to pay themselves first and then have nothing left at the end. Get comfortable with paying yourself first. It is a strategy you must start implementing as soon as possible.

Investing Your Money

Your first goal with money is to save as much as you can. Once you have enough capital, then it is time to start investing too. Investing gives you the potential to grow your money at a faster rate than just saving it. It is a great way to build your wealth throughout life.

The first thing you want to do is reinvest into your business to help it grow and prosper. This means that you should take some of your income and put it back into your various side hustles or work. For example, if you are doing lawn care, purchase higher quality equipment so that you can work on more lawns throughout the day. You can even set up a separate business bank account solely to buy things for your business. You may also place the income you receive from your businesses into this account. This will allow you to keep better track of your finances for tax purposes as well.

There are several safe investment accounts that young students can open up. If you are a minor, you will have to open a joint account with your parents. These accounts include Roth IRAs and index funds. Both serve as passive investment accounts that allow your money to grow at a faster rate than a regular bank account without you having to do much at all. These types of accounts are asset-based, which means the money you put in is distributed throughout various security assets, like stocks, bonds, real estate, and cash.

Since your money is spread throughout these various asset classes, it is a much less risky investment strategy than playing individual stocks or purchasing real estate yourself. Once you have enough capital from saving your money, consider starting one of these accounts.

You can open an investment account through a bank or brokerage firm with the help of a financial planner. The financial planner will also oversee your account and reshape it as necessary to make sure you receive the best returns on your investment. Your main goal with these accounts is to work with your financial advisor to determine what percentage of your funds will go in each asset class. The riskier accounts generally have a higher return on investment. The riskier the account, the higher the chances for gains and losses. Contribute money regularly to these accounts so they can continue to grow. Here is a breakdown of how your funds may be distributed.

- Stocks: 40%
- Bonds: 20%
- Cash: 10%
- Real estate: 30%

The main difference between different investment accounts is how they are managed and how they are taxed. Your financial advisor can fill you in on all of this. Your best bet is to go with an established company.

The point I am making here is that your money is valuable. It is hard-earned and the last thing you want to do is waste it by spending irresponsibly. This is completely avoidable if you just change a few money habits. Keep more of your own money by learning to save and invest.

Conclusion

Congratulations on making it to the end of this book, *How to Make Money in High School and College: Best Money Making Methods as a Teen, Building Your Own Apps, Selling E-books, and More Easy Side Job Ideas.* My goal for this book was to introduce to you, the readers, many new ways of making money through avenues you may have never thought of. While the subject matter is geared towards teenagers and young adults, people in their 30s, 40s, and beyond can also benefit from the information provided. Don't let the title fool you too much.

The traditional way of making an income by relying on only one source is slowly going by the wayside. There are numerous opportunities out there for people to make extra income while enjoying a flexible schedule. Also, being able to have multiple sources of income through so many different channels is a blessing for sure. My goal with this book was to introduce you to many different ways you can earn an income while going to school full time in high school and college.

Unfortunately, being a student will not allow you to get a traditional 9-5 job due to the class schedule and school work that you have to deal with. With these non-traditional forms of income, students can make some extra money on the side while still being able to focus on school full time. In some cases, you may be able to earn a full-time income and beyond, even if you are not putting in full-time hours.

Through the various lists of money-making ideas, I hope that you were able to get your creative juices going and think of many ways in your own life that can provide you with some extra cash. You certainly do not have to limit yourself to the options I provided. They are merely suggestions, but definitely something to look into. I tried to make the ideas as diverse as possible to make sure not to exclude anybody. We all have different talents and once we start recognizing them, we can open up a whole world for ourselves. Sometimes, it just takes a little extra motivation, and I am happy to provide that for you.

Throughout the different chapters, I provided an overview of the many ideas that exist out there. For the ones you found to be enticing, definitely do further research. I want you to be as informed as possible, and the main goal of this book was to give you many wide-ranging ideas.

I want to remind you that your skills are valuable. Do not be afraid to charge what you are worth, but try not to take advantage of people. It is a balance and the fairness needs to go both ways. Make sure always to set up your payment platforms so you can start accepting money right away. You do not want to start working and have no way of getting paid. That would defeat the purpose of this whole new route. Always remember to pay your taxes. Definitely keep good records of your business expenses and income. Any income you bring in is taxable. The last thing you want is to deal with the IRS. That is all I will be saying about that.

Finally, once you start bringing in extra money, make sure you are managing it responsibly. It does not matter how much you make if you do not keep any of it. I want you to hold onto as much of your money as you can. My recommendation is to set up your savings and checking account ahead of time and use the "pay yourself first" strategy to load up these accounts with your money. Once you have saved up enough, consider opening some long-term investment accounts too. The sooner in your life that you begin to save and invest, the better financial outcomes you will have for the future.

I hope this book served you well and provided you with a lot of new knowledge you never had before. It is hard to be a high school or college student and not having your own money to use for the things you want. By learning these unique methods to increase your income, you can significantly increase your independence too. Thank you for taking the time to read this book. If you enjoyed it and feel it can help other people, then please write a review, so more people become aware of it. If the information provided here helps as many people as possible, then this book is a true success. One of the keywords throughout the book is "Hustle." If you are ready to hustle, then you will likely be successful!

Join our inner circle

to sign for exclusive bonuses and free offers, including:

- Notification of new releases
- Free audiobooks
- Giveaways
- pre-release specials
- Private Facebook group access
- Video training

References

Brouhard, R. (2019, April 29). How to Become a CPR Instructor. www.thebalancecareers.com/how-do-i-become-a-cpr-instructor-1298464

Bryson, M. (2018, January 26). How to Confidently Negotiate Your Rates as a Freelancer. millo.co/confidently-negotiate-rates-freelancer

Cattanach, J. (2019, August 12). How to Become a Freelance Writer: A Newbie's to Earn Money Writing. thewritelife.com/how-to-become-a-freelance-writer/

Cabler, J. (2013, June 3). Money Making Idea #3-Detailing Cars. www.cfinancialfreedom.com/money-making-idea-3-detailing-cars

Car Wash Business: Understanding the Pros and Cons. (2012, January 2). www.detailxperts.net/blog/2012/01/02/car-wash-business-understanding-the-pros-and-cons

Clark, M. (2020). 5 Biggest Challenges Of Being A Dog Walker. dogtime.com/lifestyle/21501-biggest-challenges-dog-walker

Cooper, P. (2019, August 8). How to Make Money on Youtube: 6 Effective strategies. blog.hootsuite.com/how-to-make-money-on-youtube/

Desmond, C. (2020). This Guy's Weekend Side Job Helps Him Earn Over 2K Each Summer. www.thepennyhoarder.com/make-money/side-gigs/summer-job-caddying/

Eden, A. (2019, April 2). Flea Market Flipping: Make Money Flipping Items For Profit. www.mintnotion.com/extra-income/flea-market-flipping-make-money-flipping-items-for-profit/

Edmonson, B. (2019, July 16). How to Start Affiliate Marketing. www.thebalancesmb.com/launching-affiliate-marketing-business-2531501

Elrick, L. (2017, September 19). Industry Experts Share the True Pros and Cons of Being a Graphic Designer. www.rasmussen.edu/degrees/design/blog/pros-and-cons-of-being-graphic-designer/

Ever, T. (2017, November 24). How to successfully Sell your Photos Online as a Photographer. graphpaperpress.com/blog/sell-photos-online/

Ferreira, N.M. (2020, March 12). 10 Best Side Hustle Ideas to Make an Extra $1,000 a Month. www.oberlo.com/blog/side-hustle

Foy, K. (2017, July 5). 7 Reasons Babysitting is the Perfect Side Hustle No Matter What Your Career is. hellogiggles.com/lifestyle/money-career/reasons-babysitting-is-the-perfect-side-hustle-no-matter-what-your-career-is/

Friedman, Z. (2020, February 3). *Student Loan Debt Statistics In 2020: A Record $1.6 Trillion.* Forbes. https://www.forbes.com/sites/zackfriedman/2020/02/03/student-loan-debt-statistics/#20979d01281f

Fuller, J. (2019, October 14). 7 Jobs at the Golf Course You Should Find Interesting. www.careermetis.com/golf-course-jobs-you-should-find-interesting/

Gojko, E. (2009, September 3). House Sitting for Your Neighbor: The Dos and Don'ts. ohmyapt.apartmentratings.com/house-sitting-for-your-neighbor-the-dos-and-donts.html

Hart, K. (2018). Why Caddying is a Great Job for High School Students. caddienow.com/why-caddying-is-a-great-job-for-high-school-students/

Hayes, J. (2020). Side Hustle Series No. 1-Freelance Graphic Design. www.jenhayes.me/side-hustle-series-no-1-freelance-graphic-design

Hunt, M. (2017, September 11) 10 Money-Making Side Hustles You Can Start for Free or Cheaply. www.entrepreneur.com/article/300024

Inetwork. (2018, July 27). 4 Fundamentals of Being a Youths Sports Referee. www.leaguenetwork.com/2018/07/4-fundamentals-of-being-a-youth-sports-referee/

Jobstreet.com. (2018, December 2). Freelancing Tips for Beginners: Building Your Credibility 101.

Jorgovan, J. (2019, February 12). Pricing 101: How to Price Yourself as a Freelancer. http://careerfoundry.com/en/blog/career-change/pricing-freelancer/

Kamariya, P. (2020). YouTube as a Career: Pros and Cons. vidooly.com/blog/youtube-as-a-career-pros-cons/

Kennedy, J. (2019, August 5). How to Become a Successful Tutor. www.care.com/c/stories/5383/how-to-become-a-successful-tutor/

Knapp, J. (2019, December 16). How to Start a Blog-Beginners Guide for 2020.

www.bloggingbasics101.com/how-do-i-start-a-blog

Marinov, V. (2019, March 21). 5 Must-Have Clauses for any Freelancer Contract. www.freelancermap.com/blog/5-must-have-clauses-for-any-freelancer-contract/

Music & Arts. (2018, April 26). How to Become a Private Music Teacher. http://thevault.musicarts.com/how-to-become-private-music-teacher/

Muller, C. (2020, May 12). How to Save Money as a Teen. https://www.moneyunder30.com/how-teens-can-save-money

Muller, C. (2020, May 25). 8 Ways to Get Your Teen to Start Investing. www.doughroller.net/investing/best-investments-for-teens/

Narumanchi, S. (2020, February 12). 8 Trusted Ways to Get House Sitting Jobs. crowdworknews.com/house-sitting-jobs/

Oberlo. (N.D.) What is Dropshipping? www.oberlo.com/ebooks/dropshipping/what-is-dropshipping

Philpott, L. (N.D.). Pros & Cons of Being a Dog Walker. www.petprofessional.com.au/info-centre/pros-cons-of-being-a-dog-walker

Ransbiz. (2017). 3 Disadvantages of Domain Flipping. www.ransbiz.com/2016/07/3-disadvantages-of-domain-flipping.html

Ransbiz. (2017). 7 Advantages of Flipping Domains as an Online Business. www.ransbiz.com/2016/06/7-advantages-of-flipping-domains-as.html

Schroeder-Garndner, M. (2018, May 30). 6 Actions to Take to Find Your First Customers When No one Knows You. www.makingsenseofcents.com/2018/05/how-to-find-customers-for-your-side-hustle.html

Saxena, P. 2020, May 20. How Much Money Can You Earn Through An App? Read Here. appinventiv.com/blog/how-much-money-can-you-earn-through-your-mobile-app/

Shain, S. (2019, September 23). Calling All Homemakers: Here's How to Earn Money Selling Your Treats. www.thepennyhoarder.com/make-money/side-gigs/selling-baked-goods-from-home/

Shoes For Crews Europe. (2020, May 19) The Honest Truth: What is it Like Working in a Fast Food Restaurant. blog.sfceurope.com/what-is-it-like-working-in-a-fast-food-restaurant

SideHustleHQ. (2016). How To Start a Lawn Care Business. sidehustlehq.com/how-to-start-a-lawn-care-business/

SideHustleHQ. (2016). Making Money Buying and Selling Domain Names. sidehustlehq.com/making-money-buying-and-selling-domain-names/

Slingerland, C. (2019, December 20). How to Create an Ebook from Scratch in 2020. moosend.com/blog/how-to-create-an-eBook/

Suggett, P. (2019, November 29). Charging the Rate You Deserve as a Freelancer. www.thebalancecareers.com/freelancing-charge-the-rate-you-deserve-38878

Torres, L. (2020). Retail Workers' Biggest Challenges, Experts Advice From the Sales Floor. www.monster.com/career-advice/article/retail-workers-biggest-challenges-and-expert-advice-from-the-sales-floor

USA Today Classifieds. (N.D.). How To Work As A Lifeguard On Your Summer Break. classifieds.usatoday.com/blog/careers/work-lifeguard-summer-break/

Vaynerchuk, G. (2019). 6 Garage Sale Flipping Strategies to Make Extra Money. www.garyvaynerchuk.com/garage-sale-flipping/

Varshneya, R. (2019 June 13). A Step-by-Step Guide to Building Your First Mobile App. www.entrepreneur.com/article/231145

Ward, S. (2019, June 25). 7 Ways to Make Sure You're Getting Paid By Customers and Clients. www.thebalancesmb.com/how-to-bill-a-customer-2948033

Winn, R. (2013, May 13). How to Start a Podcast: A Complete Step-by-Step Tutorial. www.podcastinsights.com/start-a-podcast/

Witmer, D. (2019, October 29). Teens and Income Tax. /www.thebalance.com/teens-and-income-taxes-2610240

Made in the USA
Middletown, DE
14 February 2021